Contents

Foreword

Medical leadership means different things to different people in different contexts. Leaders exist because they have people following them who are able to see the vision and the courage that leaders bring with them. Sir John Tooke in his admirable report following the MTAS debacle in England highlighted that one of the reasons for the crisis was a lack of medical leadership. Lord Darzi, the then health minister, also saw this as an important issue.

Are leaders born or made? How is leadership different from management? Who leads and why? What is management? What is administration? In secondary care settings the role of medical managers is crucial in setting the agendas for service planning, quality improvement and service delivery, ensuring that services remain patient-focused and patients and their families are satisfied with the services they receive. Leaders do the right thing in spite of challenges and they have the vision, courage and passion along with a style of communication that allows them to take people with them. Managers do things right but the agenda may not be set by them. Medical leadership brings with it responsibility of improving clinical services, education, research and training. Medical leadership has many facets and skills.

This practical book is full of nuggets of wisdom of practical advice and theoretical underpinnings. I am sure medical professionals will find this of immense value and use in their day-to-day activities.

Professor Dinesh Bhugra

MA, MSc, MBBS, FRCP, FRCPsych, MPhil, PhD, FFPH

President, Royal College of Psychiatrists

May 2011

Preface

Doctors are involved in health service management and leadership at all levels. We wanted to write a book that would help them to deal effectively with the common issues they face. Our intention was to write from our own experience, drawing on the management literature we had found useful. We wanted to write something that offered learning through practical experience and so we have included many examples and exercises to ground theory in day-to-day reality. We think the exercises are important and would encourage readers to try them, modifying them where necessary to fit with their own context.

The authors have experience in coaching and mentoring medical managers and we are grateful to those we have coached and mentored for all they have taught us. We asked a panel of doctors, including several medical directors, the head of a deanery postgraduate school of psychiatry and a senior trainee to read through a draft of the book and we are grateful to Drs Wendy Burn, Suresh Chari, Kate Kucharska-Pietura, Ken McDonald and to Dr Jayanthi Devi Subramani, for their helpful comments and constructive criticism. We took their comments into account in the final draft of the book, but of course responsibility for opinions expressed and for any errors remains with the authors.

Because this is a practical book it had to be grounded in practice. The practical context is mental health services within the English National Health Service. We have, however, designed the structure, examples, exercises and approach of the text in a way that we believe will find wide applicability not only within UK mental health services but more widely in all areas of medicine and in different health systems. How far we have achieved our objectives is for you, the reader, to judge.

John Wattis
Stephen Curran
May 2011

About the authors

John Wattis is Professor of Old Age Psychiatry, University of Huddersfield. John was full time Medical Director for Leeds Community and Mental Health NHS Trust from 1995–99. He also held senior offices within the Faculty for Old Age Psychiatry of the Royal College of Psychiatrists. He has been R&D director for several NHS trusts. Before his retirement from his consultant post in the NHS, he trained as a business and life coach. Since then he has continued in his visiting university post, lecturing various student groups and supporting research. He has taught basic and advanced coaching skills to psychiatrists through the Royal College of Psychiatrists Education and Training Centre, and coached a number of NHS, university and voluntary sector staff, mostly in senior management positions. He has also acted for several years as part-time medical director (mental health) to two primary care trusts and continues to give medical management support on an *ad hoc* basis to these trusts.

Stephen Curran is Professor of Old Age Psychiatry, University of Huddersfield and Consultant in Old Age Psychiatry, Fieldhead Hospital, Wakefield. Stephen trained in Leeds and worked as Lecturer in Old Age Psychiatry at the University of Leeds until he took up his current post as Consultant in Old Age Psychiatry in Wakefield in 1998. As well as running a busy old-age psychiatry service he is also lead clinician for the Wakefield Memory Service. Stephen was also the Associate Medical Director for Education and Training for the South West Yorkshire Partnership NHS Foundation Trust from 2003–08. He was then appointed as Associate Medical Director for Old Age Psychiatry and from July 2010 has been Head of service. Stephen has contributed to significant changes in the organisation including service development and changes to the medical management arrangements. He also has considerable practical experience of dealing with the many management issues that arise in a busy old-age psychiatry service including job planning, appraisal, change management and dealing with complaints, conflicts and the pressures caused by limited resources.

CHAPTER 1

Introduction

Begin with the end in mind.

Stephen Covey[1]

DEVELOPING MANAGEMENT AND LEADERSHIP SKILLS

This book aims to be a practical introduction to the topic of medical management. Our purpose in writing this is to provide an easy-to-use guide for doctors in any kind of management role including those preparing for their first consultant or general practice principal post. We also want to help those moving into more senior medical management posts to take stock and apply their knowledge and skills in a new setting. Our approach is rooted in our experience in various clinical, academic and management posts in the English National Health Service (NHS) and universities. However, in view of the constant change in this and other health systems we have sought to keep the text open to wide application. We have also been selective in our reference to the ever-developing management literature, aiming for approaches that we know from experience work in practice. Because this is a practical guide, we have included examples and exercises to support readers in applying the knowledge and skills covered to their own situation. Hopefully readers will not only increase their competence as managers, they will also increase their enjoyment.

UNDERSTANDING THE DIFFERENCES BETWEEN ADMINISTRATION, MANAGEMENT AND LEADERSHIP

The distinction between administration, management and leadership is a vital starting point (Box 1.1). Confusion between them leads to wasted time and even to conflict.

BOX 1.1 The distinction between administration, management and leadership

Administration: Doing routine tasks well.
Management: Making things happen (often complex things in complex environments).
Leadership: Developing shared vision and direction towards a common goal or purpose and getting the best out of people in serving that purpose.

Good *administration* is doing routine tasks well. A bureaucratic approach works well here (*see* later section on *management cultures and cultural appropriateness* in Chapter 3). *Management* involves making things happen even when the environment is not simple and the tasks themselves may be complicated. It requires attention to detail and often involves teamwork. *Leadership* means helping a group or organisation to find its direction and drawing the best out of people to serve a common purpose. Leadership motivates teams to work well.

Good administration is essential but nobody should employ an expensive doctor to do simple, straightforward administrative tasks. On occasion we still hear of doctors doing their own typing or filing for lack of adequate secretarial support. (There is no problem in this for those doctors who have excellent keyboard skills and are supported by effective software and computer systems. However, too often doctors who do not have these skills are expected to act as typists when this is not a 'core skill'. Lack of adequate computer systems, software and support result in the wastage of many hours of expensive medical time. This can mean doctors working unpaid overtime and/or employers wasting medical competencies and using doctors inefficiently.)

Modern medical practice is largely delivered by teamwork and so any consultant or principal in general practice will need at least a basic level of competency in management and leadership skills. Many newly appointed consultants and principals in general practice feel they have not acquired this basic level of competency through their training, which has understandably been focused on producing *competent clinicians*.

Those aspiring to more senior management roles as clinical directors, medical directors, associate medical directors and to managerial roles in medical education will require much more than basic competency. Until recently the development of higher levels of competency in these areas has been on an *ad hoc* basis; although, for example, the British Association of Medical Managers developed its own 'Fit to Lead' programme with associated standards and competencies. These covered these areas:

➤ communication
➤ developing people
➤ developing the business
➤ developing self
➤ the wider contexts
➤ quality.

The British Medical Journal/Open University Clinical Leadership Programme covers similar topics (http://clinicalleadership.bmj.com/student).These competencies are also covered in this book.

Doctors in senior management positions (such as medical directors), most of whom choose to continue in clinical practice, have the unenviable task of keeping up to date in both management and in their chosen area of clinical practice. Generally continued involvement in clinical work by doctors in senior management roles helps them to keep in touch *and be seen to keep in touch* with clinical reality (*see* Chapter 5). There is enormous value in senior practising clinicians being involved in management, medical education and professional leadership. In senior medical management positions the art is to design any involvement in clinical work, with the help of colleagues, in such a way that it is circumscribed so that interference in either direction between different roles is minimised. 'Protected time' for both clinical and management roles is vital and should be recognised as such by employers.

Leadership and management *can* be distinguished but the relationship between them in successful organisations is close. Leadership defines direction, enables, empowers and even inspires, but without management competency *it does not deliver*. The words we use to define management roles for doctors in the NHS demonstrate the complex interactions between 'direction', leadership and management:

➤ Medical director (usually an *executive* director post)
➤ Associate medical director
➤ Clinical director (often providing a lead and supported by a manager)
➤ Clinical lead (not the same as clinical director or clinical leader)
➤ Team leader (sometimes the team 'manager' rather than the leader).

Virtually all medical managers need also to be good leaders. But they have to work within a context of direction set by their organisation and that can sometimes cause conflict. Public service management is out of fashion at present and there is a tendency for modern management theory and practice to come from the commercial sector where the 'bottom line' is the bottom line of shareholder profit. Hopefully, following the market failures of 2008, an appropriate re-emphasis on public service management and its values will eventually emerge.

Clarity about roles and what titles mean is important. If a service has a clinical *lead* and a non-medical *manager*; who defines the *direction*? (*See* Box 1.2.)

BOX 1.2 Conflict between management and leadership due to lack of clarity

A new specialist service is set up. A service manager is appointed but the job description contains no reference to the relationship with the 'clinical lead'. The doctor appointed to clinical lead is unsure of his/her relationship to the manager. Normally leadership sets the direction and management achieves the desired outcomes. Here it is different. The manager is heavily 'performance managed' (from above) according to national and locally determined 'targets'. So what is the role of the clinical lead? At one extreme it could simply be to 'advise' the manager about clinical issues (so why not 'clinical advisor'?) or to 'lead' the clinical aspects of the service along a direction determined by others; at the other it could be to innovate and inspire and give direction to the manager and the team. This can only be resolved by careful negotiation and explicit agreement between the manager and the clinical lead. This will need to involve more senior management and take into account the views of other members of the team. Failure to resolve leads to conflict and inefficiency.

EXERCISE 1.1

Using three columns make a list of the administrative, management and leadership components of your ('management') job. Eliminate any tasks in the administrative column (as far as possible) by delegation to others (secretary, management assistant, personnel officer, etc.). If you have nobody appropriate to delegate to, ask how and when such support can be developed and make it a priority. Now look at the largely leadership and management tasks that remain and put them into priority order. Decide how and when you will make time for the priority tasks. (The rationale for this can be seen in Stephen Covey's bestselling management book, *The Seven Habits of Highly Effective People*.[1] This task has elements of the first three habits: being proactive, beginning with the end in mind and putting first things first.)

CORE COMPETENCIES OF MANAGERS AND LEADERS

Table 1.1 gives a list of some of the skills or competencies that medical managers and leaders need (a couple of rows are blank for you to add your own ideas).

TABLE 1.1 Some competencies of managers and leaders

Management	Leadership
Negotiation	Setting direction
Change management	Enabling
Supervision	Empowering
Conflict resolution	Involving
Delegation	Inspiring
Communicating information	Listening
Giving feedback	Influencing
Dealing with crises	Avoiding crises
Performance management	Leading by example

The trainee in medicine will have experience in a number of these skills. What doctor, in a modern health service, has not had to negotiate with patients and carers over treatment plans or with colleagues over on-call or leave arrangements? We have all seen change managed (almost constantly in the modern NHS and not always well). All doctors in training should have had clinical and educational supervision. They will almost certainly have been involved in conflict resolution and crisis management and will have been the object of much delegation! They may not have had so much experience in setting direction; but, if they have been lucky in their training experience, they will have been supervised by consultants who were enabling, empowering, involving and even inspiring. Inevitably they will have been influenced by the examples (not always good) of those with whom they have trained.

Many new consultants will feel that they have not had enough systematic teaching or practical experience in these areas, though this, like the support for those taking more senior management roles, is improving.

EXERCISE 1.2

In two columns (one for management and one for leadership) make a list of the competencies you believe you require for management and leadership in your current role. Rate yourself on a scale of 1 (poor) to 5 (excellent) in each competency. If you have trusted colleagues you may wish to ask one or more of them to rate you, too, to get different perspectives. Consider how you can make the most of the areas you are rated highly on and determine how important it is to improve any other areas. If it is important make a plan to do something about these areas.

Achievement demands synergy between leadership and management. The Duke of Wellington was a great military leader but historians attribute some of his success to attention to detail in managing the logistics of his military operations. Inspired decisions on the battlefield were supported by months of careful preparation, despite the *administrative* tasks imposed by the central bureaucracy against which he sometimes rebelled (Box 1.3).

BOX 1.3 Duke of Wellington's Dispatch to Whitehall (displayed at Mirehouses, the country home of one of his descendants in Cumbria)

August 1812

Gentlemen,

Whilst marching from Portugal to a position that commands the approach to Madrid and the French forces, my officers have been diligently complying with your requests, which have been sent by H. M. ship from London to Lisbon and thence by dispatch rider to our headquarters.

We have enumerated our saddles, bridles, tents and tent poles, and all manner of sundry items for which His Majesty's Government holds me accountable. I have dispatched reports on the character, wit and spleen of every officer. Each item and every farthing has been accounted for, with two regrettable exceptions for which I beg your indulgence.

Unfortunately the sum of one shilling and nine pence remains unaccounted for in one infantry battalion's petty cash and there has been hideous confusion as to the number of jars of raspberry jam issued to one cavalry regiment during a sandstorm in western Spain. This reprehensible carelessness may be related to the pressure of circumstances, since we are at war with France, a fact which may come as a bit of a surprise to you gentlemen in Whitehall.

This brings me to my present purpose, which is to request elucidation of my instructions from His Majesty's Government, so that I may better understand why I am dragging an army over these barren plains. I construe that perforce it must be one of two alternative duties, as given below. I shall pursue either one with my best ability, but I cannot do both.

1   To train an army of uniformed British clerks in Spain for the benefit of the accountants and copy-boys in London, or, perchance.
2   To see to it that the forces of Napoleon are driven out of Spain.

Your most obedient servant,

Wellington.

STARTING IN A NEW SITUATION

In any new situation, whether on first appointment as a consultant, or as a medical manager of whatever grade, it is essential to start well. Handling transition to a role with increased responsibilities is never easy and it is always useful to make time to reflect on developing roles and responsibilities, preferably with the help of a mentor, coach or other level-headed person. Even if you have been in your current situation for some time it makes sense to reappraise the situation and to make a fresh start from time to time. Often this needs to be done after at least a few months spent exploring the demands and limits of the role. The areas to be appraised to achieve this fresh start can be summed up in the 'three Rs', as follows:

➤ roles
➤ relationships
➤ responsibilities.

Roles

One of the strengths of how medicine is organised is that management jobs involve continuing clinical practice (and sometimes academic and/ or training roles as well). It is useful to make an inventory of key roles. *See* Table 1.2 for an example of key roles for a newly appointed medical director. Clarity about the key roles as they develop helps to ensure that no one area is neglected or sacrificed accidentally. It also enables a continuing review of both the roles and the priority to be given to them. One of the authors has even, from time to time, colour-shaded his weekly programme according to the different roles over a period of a week to get a clearer idea of which roles were stealing the time! Be aware, if you do this, that one of the things you may find is that roles (especially administrative roles) that are not properly your own can be taking up time and that delegation is called for.

Organisations that are run by 'boards', like NHS trusts, have a mixture of executive directors in roles such as chief executive, medical director, finance director, human resources director and director of quality supported by non-executive directors chosen for their expertise in areas like accountancy, business management, local politics, etc. One of the non-executives acts as chair of the board and collectively they are responsible for providing a degree of outside scrutiny, support and common sense to guide the executive directors in their work and the board in its decision-making. Once decisions are made, the board is expected to stand behind them.

TABLE 1.2 Key roles for a newly appointed medical director

Role	Remarks
Medical advice and leadership to board	This will involve good communication with relevant medical colleagues and fair evaluation of sometimes competing priorities. It will also involve good relationships with other directors and a recognition of what they contribute.
Medical employment and disciplinary matters	Here the relationship with the director of human resources, other human resources staff, the local representatives of the British Medical Association (BMA) and the doctor's own defence union are likely to be helpful.
Leader of team of doctors	Mutual respect between members of the medical management team and senior colleagues is vital.
Continuing clinical work	For more junior management posts clinical workload may only require minor adjustment; for the most senior posts it may have to be severely limited. In either case smooth organisation and the cooperation of colleagues is essential.
Wider responsibilities	Some medical managers will also have roles within professional organisations of clinicians or of managers, or will be involved in wider health service or related work.
Other roles	At this stage it does no harm to remind oneself of the wider roles within work (e.g. teacher, researcher) and outside of work (parent, partner, participator in recreational activities, etc.).

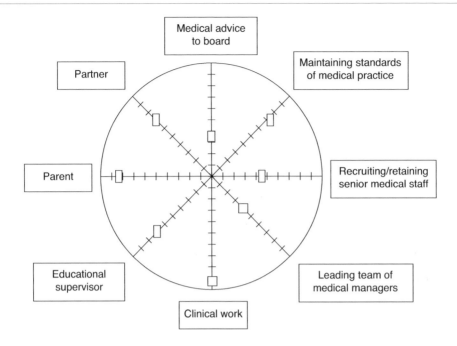

FIGURE 1.1 'Balance wheel' for the role of medical director

Figure 1.1 gives an example of how a 'balance wheel' can be used to look at the different roles, for example, of a newly appointed medical director, and how well they are being fulfilled. In this kind of a plot the subject makes a judgement about how well s/he is fulfilling each role on a scale of 0 (centre of circle) to 10 (periphery). Some people join the dots and make the point that if you end up with an odd shaped figure you are in for a 'bumpy ride'!

In this example there are 8 radii but there can be as many or as few as the situation demands. The labels applied to each radius here are roughly the same as in Table 1.2 but note that the issues of medical employment and discipline have been separated out in the table.

This tool can lead to a reappraisal of priorities. For example, the balance wheel above leads to an understanding that the issue of medical advice to the board needs urgent action. Recruitment and retention of senior medical staff and leading the team of medical managers also appear to be priorities. Review of all the information in the balance wheel might lead to an action plan, such as that outlined in Table 1.3.

TABLE 1.3 Illustrative action plan that might arise from considering the issues highlighted by the 'balance wheel' of Figure 1.1

Role	Action	Timing
Medical advice to board	Discuss with CEO	Today
Recruiting/retaining senior medical staff	Discuss with associate MDs	Next week
Maintaining standards of medical practice	Discuss (and if necessary develop) policies with other relevant directors	Before 'away day' below
Leading team of medical managers	Plan for 'away day' to develop shared vision and values	Plan now for next month
Clinical work	No action	
Educational supervisor	Explore support to trainee from another appropriate consultant	This week
Parent	Get home on time	Tonight
Partner	Don't neglect	Always

EXERCISE 1.3

Make your own list of key roles. Reflect on how important each is to you personally and to the organisation you work for. On a scale of 1–10 make a judgement on how well you fulfil each of these roles. (You can make a table, or use a balance wheel *see* Figure 1.1). Consider how you could improve your scores where necessary. This might mean reallocating time, delegating some less important tasks to others, working to get more support in a particular role or any other action for which you can take responsibility. Plan definite actions and give them timescales. Resolve to make at least one change in the week ahead and others incrementally, ideally allocating dates to start and complete each.

Relationships

Each of the roles above involves key relationships. Modern medicine is a team effort and good relationships are the foundation for effective clinical and managerial teams. Many failures in health and social services are blamed on poor communication but, as the management writer Stephen Covey points out, good communication depends on trust and trust, in turn, is based on our assessment of the other person's 'character and competence'.[1] This can be briefly expressed as a management 'equation':

Communication ~ trust = character × competence

Starting in a new job, one needs to make a list (or 'mind map') of key relation-ships. These relationships will generally relate to the roles considered earlier. For example, in making sure adequate attention is paid to medical opinion on the board, in the example above, the chief executive is a key relationship. Other directors with clinical responsibilities are also likely to be important in this context. In issues of medical staffing and discipline, the personnel director and any medical personnel specialist is likely to figure and so on.

What makes effective relationships at work? Here is a list that you may wish to expand:
➤ mutual respect
➤ shared vision (and mission)
➤ shared values
➤ clear definitions of roles and responsibilities
➤ flexibility (within limits)
➤ integrity.

Mutual respect is a great starting point, but how often do we hear doctors 'slagging off' managers or vice versa? Barack Obama, in his autobiographical treatise on reshaping American politics, *The Audacity of Hope*,[2] stressed the importance of respecting the views of others, even when we don't agree with them. This requires a degree of empathy, of willingness to see and acknowl-edge the other person's point of view. It requires spending time finding out about their values, their understanding of what motivates people and their vision for how services should run and be developed. It emphatically does not involve the lazy prejudice of always imputing the worst motives to oth-ers. We all need to understand and respect each other's positions. That is the starting point of good relationships.

Within the work context, **shared vision** is also crucial. This does not come naturally and requires hard work. It applies at all levels. The clinical team needs shared vision. The different elements of a service require shared vision. The different parts of an organisation need shared vision. At board level this vision needs to be a guiding principle that is genuinely shared not only by board members but by all managers, clinicians and other employees. Everyone in the organisation should be able to articulate what the organisation is there for (mission), where it is heading (vision) and how it intends to get there (values). Lack of such shared understanding leads to inefficiency and disrup-tion within any organisation as different factions pull in different directions. When an organisation is new, shared vision can be developed by a process that involves all staff and also takes fully into account the ideas of service users.

In practice a strong vision for future direction often comes from a chief executive or senior manager. But, however charismatic the manager, it is essential to listen to other people's points of view and to ensure, as far as possible, that all staff feel genuine 'ownership' of the vision. A doctor newly appointed to a management position needs to find out what senior managers think about the purpose and direction of the organisation. He or she may even need to help others to become clear about this.

If *mission* is what we as an organisation are there for and *vision* is about the direction we are heading in, **values** are about how we get there. What standards of behaviour are expected of us? Values can be expressed in an ethical code. The General Medical Council's (GMC's) statement on 'Duties of a Doctor'[3] (Box 1.4) is at once an expression of standards and of their underpinning values.

BOX 1.4 Duties of a doctor

Patients must be able to trust doctors with their lives and health. To justify that trust you must show respect for human life and you must:
- make the care of your patient your first concern
- protect and promote the health of patients and the public
- provide a good standard of practice and care
- keep your professional knowledge and skills up to date
- recognise and work within the limits of your competence
- work with colleagues in the ways that best serve patients' interests
- treat patients as individuals and respect their dignity
- treat patients politely and considerately
- respect patients' right to confidentiality
- work in partnership with patients
- listen to patients and respond to their concerns and preferences
- give patients the information they want or need in a way they can understand
- respect patients' right to reach decisions with you about their treatment and care
- support patients in caring for themselves to improve and maintain their health
- be honest and open and act with integrity
- act without delay if you have good reason to believe that you or a colleague may be putting patients at risk
- never discriminate unfairly against patients or colleagues
- never abuse your patients' trust in you or the public's trust in the profession.

You are personally accountable for your professional practice and must always be prepared to justify your decisions and actions.

Though the GMC publishes more detailed guidance on management for doctors,[4] this general ethical statement, with minor additions, serves as a statement of values for doctors involved in management.

Putting the patient first and wider concern for the health of the population are (or should be) what the NHS is all about. It is not just clinicians who have an obligation to provide a good standard of clinical practice and care. *Clinical governance* places that obligation on all healthcare organisations. Apart from clinical standards, management practice, too, has its standards, expressed through the duties of *corporate governance*, which covers financial and other aspects of probity. Doctors who are managers, like other managers, need to keep up to date, to recognise their limits and to 'work in partnership with colleagues', cooperating in the interest of patients (and the wider population). In some cases management concepts may be wider than clinical concepts. For example management understanding of confidentiality may also embrace concepts such as commercial confidentiality or intellectual property rights. Listening, giving necessary information, respecting employees' viewpoints (though not necessarily giving every employee the primacy the patient enjoys in the management of a medical condition) and supporting employees are all useful management values. Honesty and integrity speak for themselves.

So the ethical values of doctors and the ethical values of managers (at least in a public service organisation) can easily be aligned and compared. In commercial organisations the duty to return a profit for shareholders can appear to be in conflict with some of the other duties. This is one of the reasons that some people have reservations about the introduction of more 'for profit' companies into the provision of NHS services. Clarity is essential in this situation. In medical ethics, the other values of a healthcare organisation are equally as important as (and, in the case of 'putting patients first', more important than) 'duty to shareholders'.

Clear definitions of roles and responsibilities enable people to work efficiently and effectively without constantly 'tripping over' invisible boundaries (*see* Box 1.2). It is remarkable how often, in a complicated organisation like the NHS, definitions are unclear. This can result in much wasted effort and sometimes in bad feeling!

Flexibility (within limits) is just as important as clear boundaries. Sometimes we may choose to take on extra work outside of our normal duties. However, we should always beware of unlimited flexibility resulting in overwork or lack of clear definition or of flexibility that, ratchet-like, only works in one direction!

Integrity in the sense of being true to oneself and fair to others is an essential factor in successful management and leadership. Machiavelli's ideas notwithstanding, people work better when they know they can trust their colleagues. The multiple roles of medical managers make integrity particularly important. Great clarity of thinking and boundary setting are needed to maintain integrity (*see* Box 1.5).

BOX 1.5 Maintaining integrity

After a meeting, a consultant 'buttonholes' the medical director and asks for 'a quiet word'. The medical director takes the colleague (Dr A), who is clearly angry, to a private office. The consultant asks if he can speak about a colleague (Dr B) 'in confidence'. The medical director (who has been in similar situations before) reminds his colleague that confidentiality is always bounded. If he hears about anything where his duties as a doctor or as a manager require him to act, he will not be able to guarantee confidentiality. The colleague accepts this and, before the medical director can say more, launches into an account of his fury that Dr B has sent him an email concerning leave arrangements that he considers to be demeaning and bullying. Dr B has compounded this 'offence' by copying the email to a several colleagues.

What happens next will depend on circumstances. If this is the first time the medical director has heard of Dr B behaving in this way she might adopt a coaching or mentoring approach to help Dr A to find a way of dealing with Dr B (with or without any intervention from the medical director). If this is not the first time that such issues have surfaced and previous informal attempts to resolve them have failed, or if the email is so outrageous as to demand further action, the medical director needs to decide whether a more formal investigation and intervention is required. If this is the case, the medical director has maintained her integrity by reminding Dr A that confidentiality is always bounded.

Responsibilities

Doctors are trained to have a clear sense of personal responsibility for patients under their care. Consultants generally feel that they have the authority (though not always the resources) in the clinical situation to discharge their clinical responsibilities. Even in the clinical situation, in complex areas like psychiatry, responsibility may be shared (again, the GMC has a document[5]). However, responsibility should never be so diffuse that nobody takes it! Responsibility for ensuring the care or treatment plan is delivered may rest with the care coordinator or the case manager and it is essential that employers take responsibility for ensuring that clinicians of all disciplines have the necessary competencies to undertake tasks that they are expected to perform. Traditionally the GMC has laid on doctors the duty to ensure that anybody to whom they delegate care is competent to deliver that care. In a large multidisciplinary team this responsibility now rests with the employer. However, if doctors have doubts about the competency of colleagues, they are expected to act.

How exactly to act will depend on circumstances. It may involve talking to the colleague face to face. If the colleague is from another discipline and the matter is of serious concern it may necessitate talking to a service manager, clinical director or a manager in that particular discipline. Doctors should always have a mentor or other trusted peer to whom they can go for support in deciding what to do if they have concerns of this nature. Ultimately they should be able to consult a medical manager and/or their defence organisation for support and advice. The best course of action will depend on local structures and relationships as well as upon the nature and severity of the concern. Nobody should feel alone in dealing with this kind of situation. If they do, management has failed.

When we move away from the clinical situation to the managerial situation, responsibilities, boundaries and authority are often hard to pin down. Nevertheless it is worth the effort to obtain clarity!

To roles, responsibilities and relationships we could add a fourth 'r' – *resources*. There rarely seem to be enough to do the job as well as the well-trained professional wants. For the medical manager there is a twofold duty. First, it is imperative to make the best possible use of available resources (*efficiency*). Second, where a case can be made for extra resources it is important to prioritise need and to make an evidence-based 'business case' for the development or reallocation of resources (*equity*). Simply complaining that there is not enough is inadequate.

CONCLUSION

In this chapter we have considered the distinctions between administration, management and leadership. We have begun to look at the competencies needed to manage and lead successfully. We have suggested a framework for evaluating the roles, relationships and responsibilities of the managerial component of any medical job. In doing this we have emphasised the complexity of the roles undertaken by medical managers and the necessity for good working relationships. In the next chapter we will look more closely at key relationships and how to keep them healthy. Later chapters will examine the impact of different management cultures and the need to be able to operate efficiently in the various cultures found in any large organisation. We will examine some of the key skills and competencies that medical managers need to develop. We will look at developing and sharing personal vision and values and at maintaining personal (including 'work–life') balance. We will examine the importance of 'iteration' in developing understanding for senior managers. Cooperative ways of working and thriving in an ever-changing environment are also highlighted. Our last chapters revisit some of the earlier work on personal balance and seek to support medical managers in keeping going and knowing when to stop!

REFERENCES

1 Covey S. *The 7 Habits of Highly Effective People.* London: Simon and Schuster; 2004.
2 Obama B. *The Audacity of Hope.* Edinburgh: Canongate; 2008.
3 The General Medical Council. *Good Medical Practice.* London: GMC; 2006.
4 The General Medical Council. *Management for Doctors.* London: GMC; 2006.
5 The General Medical Council. *Accountability in Muliti-disciplinary and Multi-agency Mental Health Teams.* London: GMC; 2005.

CHAPTER 2

Maintaining productive key relationships

No man is an island . . .

John Donne (1572–1631)

The quality of our relationships underpins our achievements in life. This chapter examines in more detail some key working relationships. As well as describing healthy relationships, we also look at what can go wrong and how it can be mended. Medical school selection procedures mean that doctors are usually very intelligent in the sense that they are intellectually bright and academically accomplished. However, research on so-called emotional intelligence (EI), shows that in many areas EI is a stronger predictor of success than intellect.[1] EI has many definitions and unlike conventional intelligence it is said to be relatively easy to develop. It can be characterised as competency in interpersonal interaction based on empathy, self-awareness, self-regulation, self-motivation, social awareness and social skills. There are many questionnaires designed to measure emotional intelligence or 'emotional quotient' (EQ), somewhat analogous to intelligence quotient (IQ). Despite the fact that (rather like IQ) it is a concept with disputed boundaries and properties it nonetheless describes something that is pragmatically useful in understanding management issues.

Transactional analysis (TA – *see* Figure 2.1) is another useful framework for looking at interactions. TA, like emotional intelligence theory, recognises that we are not strictly rational beings who relate to each other in patterns determined entirely by logic. It recognises that when we interact with others we do so in ways that are as much determined by emotions and past experience as by the present facts. Like other conceptual frameworks we will use (for example organisational culture in the next chapter), TA is essentially metaphorical in nature and as such subject to many limitations.[2] Nevertheless it is a useful tool for understanding and managing our relationships on a day-to-day basis. In essence it asserts that we all have three main ego states from which we can interact with others. The parent state (P) has two 'supervisory' functions. One incorporates the nurturing side of parenthood, the other (critical parent) the 'oughts' and 'shoulds' we internalise as we grow up. Some of these may be very useful and some may be distinctly unhelpful. In this metaphor, the adult ego state (A) sees, hears, thinks and comes up with reality-based solutions to problems. The child ego state (C) is more emotional and carries emotional memories from childhood. When it is 'hooked', sometimes by the perceived 'parental' communication of a colleague, childhood emotions inappropriate to the present situation can come rushing to the fore. Like the parent function it has two subdivisions, the 'compliant' and the 'rebellious' child. Two other concepts from TA are useful in understanding the social psychology of human interaction. One is the idea of 'crossed' transactions, when, for example, one person communicates on an A–A level but the other perceives the comment as critical and responds with a

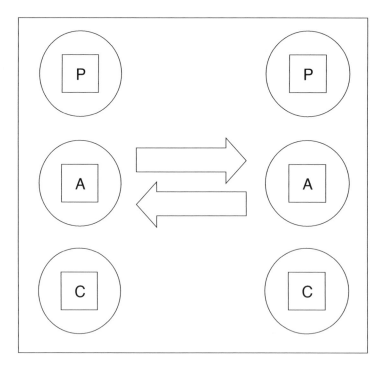

FIGURE 2.1 Parent (P), Adult (A) and Child (C) ego states as envisaged in TA: A–A transaction illustrated

C–P communication. An example might be 'How long have we got to discuss this situation?' (A–A) with the response 'Why are you always rushing me?' (C–P). The other useful idea is that we all have 'scripts', which are learned ways of dealing with situations. Again these are sometimes useful, sometimes not and, even when useful, may impede our flexibility. An excellent brief introduction to TA has been written by Carol Solomon.[3]

Equipped with these tools, let us look at some of the key interactions of doctors in management roles.

RELATIONSHIPS IN THE MULTIDISCIPLINARY TEAM

Perhaps the first really important 'leadership' role at work for many doctors is that of consultant working in a multi-disciplinary team. This is often not a well-defined role and difficulties can easily arise. One of the commonest causes of difficulty is different expectations (*see* Box 2.1).

BOX 2.1 A case of different expectations

A doctor is appointed to replace a consultant colleague who has just retired early. The new consultant has a consensual style of leadership. He shares the ward with another consultant who is more authoritarian. He finds that ward staff are constantly asking his secretary to fix appointments for him to speak to patients' relatives. On a number of occasions relatives are somewhat apologetic, explaining that they only wanted a 'progress report' and didn't need to 'bother' the consultant. Looking at his ever-more crammed schedule the doctor decides that he needs to develop a 'screening' system so that when relatives ask for information, they get it from the primary nurse or the ward doctor in the first instance and are only referred to the consultant if the issue is particularly difficult. The doctor decides to discuss his ideas first with the senior consultant. The senior colleague explains that she has tried to implement such a system for the last five years without success. Nurses have always resisted her plans for them to deal with things directly but she is willing to back up her new colleague if he wants to 'have a go'. The new consultant makes an appointment to talk to the senior ward manager. He lays before her the issue of his diary not having enough space to see so many relatives and asks if she has any ideas to support him in dealing with the issue. She says that his predecessor always wanted to see relatives personally and did not trust nurses to 'give out information'. He tries again, asking what the ward manager thinks. She says the other consultant on the ward would need to agree to any change in 'policy'. The new consultant says he thinks he can deliver that and proposes a 'triage' system where the appropriate nurse from the primary nursing team takes all queries from relatives and decides whether to deal with them by herself, to deal with them jointly with the junior doctor or to refer to the consultant. There is always the option to involve the consultant if necessary. After further negotiation and some training for the staff this scheme is successfully implemented (and the consultant's schedule is less crowded).

The example above can be understood using concepts from both EI and TA. The emotional intelligence of the new consultant is demonstrated in several ways. He does not react to the situation by raving about the impossibility of fitting so much into his diary but looks for the causes of the situation. Once he has understood the source of the problem he considers possible options but then realises he does not want to go ahead without understanding the position of his senior colleague. Having done this he approaches the ward manager in what in TA terms is an 'adult–adult' communication. She does not respond directly to his approach but reacts in what is essentially a 'child–parent' way. He does not allow himself to be 'hooked' into criticising his retired colleague, nor does he snap back 'Well, I'm different' but asks again for her thoughts. Again she responds defensively but, because he has prepared well, he is able to reassure her and propose a clear way of dealing with the situation. It is not put into effect immediately (culture change is rarely rapid) but after further negotiation and training the proposal is implemented successfully.

Another insight from TA is useful here. It is not only individuals who have 'scripts' (habitual ways of dealing with things based on past experience); organisations, too, tend to deal with things in the way they have always done. Different professions also may typically have different perspectives on how the multi-disciplinary team works. Some of these are *stereotypes* and need to be shifted if genuine cooperation is to flourish. At a lecture reporting a study on multidisciplinary working in forensic psychiatry, an academic from a nursing background suggested to the speaker that the problems were all due to the behaviour of doctors and the medical model. The sociologist who was giving the lecture refused to affirm this prejudice! It is important to bring any maladaptive beliefs about authority and responsibility in the team into the open in a way that encourages respectful adult–adult communication and resolution. Unless we agree about our purpose, vision and values, we are unlikely to function well together. It is a function of leadership to facilitate this agreement. Interestingly, management research shows that 'followers' put *trust, compassion, stability and hope* ahead of vision as qualities they wanted in leaders.[4] Trust and compassion are clearly functions of good (emotionally intelligent, adult–adult) relationships.

EXERCISE 2.1

(If you don't work in a multidisciplinary clinical or management team or you work in one where everyone always works well together you can skip this one!) Look at the team you work in and select an area where there seems to be misunderstandings between yourself and other team members. Seek to understand their position and where it originates (you may need to listen to them to achieve this!). See whether you can jointly understand the source of the problems and find some solutions (you may need to involve others). Agree on a plan to implement the solutions, and on how you will all know you have succeeded. Agree a time to review progress.

We are not suggesting that all problems can always be solved by an individual taking action. In fact, in a complicated organisation, individuals often need to enlist others if they are going to make a real and lasting difference.

Sometimes, the cooperative approach may not work with an individual or group from a different discipline. If there are important differences that cannot be resolved on an informal face-to-face basis, one has to consider the other options. These should generally be discussed with a respected and experienced colleague. They may involve working with an individual's line manager, or seeking sponsorship for developmental work with the other person or the group, led by an appropriately skilled facilitator. One thing is certain, if an important relationship within the clinical team is dysfunctional, it does not pay to ignore it. If we avoid the problem we may allow it to become worse (and harder to deal with when we can avoid it no longer).

So far we have looked at how we deal with problems. We can reduce the frequency of problems by adhering to the principles of good relationships outlined in Chapter 1:
➤ mutual respect
➤ shared vision (and mission)
➤ shared values
➤ clear definitions of roles and responsibilities
➤ flexibility (within limits)
➤ integrity.

It pays to build good relationships. In the context of family relationships Steven Covey writes of 'building the emotional bank account'.[5] *Genuine* interest in others and their points of view, acknowledgement of their skills and competencies and a respectful attitude where there is genuine disagreement will do a lot to build team cohesion. Some of the approaches used in coaching (*see* Chapter 5) are helpful here.

Relationships with doctors

There are many different kinds of working relationships between doctors (this list aims to be illustrative rather than exhaustive):

➤ master–apprentice
➤ educational supervisor/clinical supervisor–student/trainee
➤ peer relationships (e.g. between a group of primary care doctors and/or consultants)
➤ clinical director–specialist consultant–specialty doctor
➤ medical director–clinical director–consultant

We have put 'master–apprentice' first because medicine is an ancient profession and (certainly up until recently) there have been strong elements of the old 'master–apprentice' relationship in training. The idea of consultant or principal in primary care medicine as 'master' of his or her craft is still present and explains the way in which consultants and principals in general practice still sometimes tend to regard themselves as independent 'craftsmen'. The 'apprenticeship' model is still often used to apply to learning in the clinical situation. This is not the place to go into the attitudes and practices (some helpful, some not) that still survive from the 'master–apprentice' era. However, it is well to remember that this is still relatively recent history and still affects how people behave. There are also overlaps with the 'club' culture (the masters are all members of the 'club') and the 'craft' culture discussed in the next chapter.

Supervisory and educational relationships

Nobody now learns to be a doctor by staying with one master of a particular branch of the craft for many years. Instead we have a highly structured university curriculum for undergraduates and complicated training schemes for various 'specialties'. Most doctors, even in their training years, will have had some involvement with medical students. When they become consultants they will often take on a new role as an educational or clinical supervisor of doctors in training. They will have had this role 'modelled' for them during their own training and, especially with recent changes in the format and assessment of postgraduate training, they are likely themselves to have had some special training for this role. Although not the only skill set needed for educational supervision, many of the skills used in coaching (Chapter 5) are relevant here.

In the UK the roles of educational and clinical supervisor have been redefined by the Postgraduate Medical Education and Training Board (the PMETB was set up in 2003 and has been merged with the GMC since April 2010). Box 2.2 reproduces these definitions.

BOX 2.2 PMETB/GMC definitions of clinical and educational supervisors (see www.gmc-uk.org/Briefing_Note_Two_2010.pdf_30511703. pdf)

Clinical supervisor: 'A trainer who is selected and appropriately trained to be responsible for overseeing a specified trainee's clinical work and providing constructive feedback during a training placement. Some training schemes appoint an educational supervisor for each placement. The roles of clinical and educational supervisor may then be merged'.

Educational supervisor: 'A trainer who is selected and appropriately trained to be responsible for the overall supervision and management of a specified trainee's educational progress during a training placement or series of placements. The educational supervisor is responsible for the trainee's educational agreement'.

In psychiatry the educational supervisor and the clinical supervisor are usually the same person. The advantage of this arrangement is that there is no disjunction between clinical and educational supervision. The potential disadvantage is that in the case of personality clash or disagreement with the clinical supervisor, the trainee cannot turn to the educational supervisor. However, there is usually a college tutor or scheme organiser who can fill this role. Broadly speaking, for most doctors, supervisory relationships have two main components. One is developmental (epitomised by coaching skills), the other involves clinical supervision and, increasingly, assessment. There can be tensions between these roles but all are important. If the developmental role is handled skilfully, the supervisory role is usually less burdensome and assessment less threatening. We are responsible for our students and doctors in training, especially for ensuring we do not delegate to them tasks beyond their present competence. It scarcely seems possible that one of the authors did locums while still a medical student, when he was expected to help 'cover' casualty! Fortunately we have moved on since then and the problems in training today tend to be in the opposite direction with the need to make sure that trainees are sufficiently 'stretched' and gain sufficient breadth of clinical experience gradually to develop sound independent clinical judgement.

The clinical and educational supervisors are also responsible for identifying issues of underperformance and dealing with them. The supervisor will generally do this with the support of the appropriate medical personnel/human resources department and in collaboration with a college tutor, training-scheme organiser or other experienced colleague appointed by the deanery. Minor issues can be dealt with locally but if they cannot be resolved in a satisfactory way then deanery-appointed colleagues must become involved (*see* Box 2.3).

BOX 2.3 Resolving performance difficulties with doctors in training

Dr Jones had been appointed as a senior trainee in psychiatry. She had done well in her interview. No concerns were raised and her references were very good. The first year of her training was uneventful. During her second year of training a number of minor issues were raised. She was arriving late at work more often and needed to be reminded about completing letters. There were also increasing errors on prescriptions, one resulting in a formal investigation by the pharmacy department when amoxycillin was prescribed to a patient allergic to penicillin. The clinical/educational supervisor had a meeting with Dr Jones but no specific issues were identified. The problems continued and seemed to worsen so after consultation Dr Jones agreed to meet the local college tutor but again no progress was at first made in relation to trying to understand the underlying problem. After a number of meetings with the tutor Dr Jones admitted that she didn't feel 'well' but didn't want to discuss it with local doctors because she was worried that she 'might lose her job'. She was encouraged to go and see her GP but in addition an appointment was made for her to discuss her situation with the programme director for the scheme at the local deanery. The meeting at the deanery proved very successful. Dr Jones explained that she had had a recent bereavement and was feeling low in mood but had felt concerned about discussing this with her consultant (who was both the clinical and educational supervisor) as she felt it might affect her future reference. She agreed to see her GP and her wish not to discuss this with local colleagues was respected.

In the UK, the 'specialty grade' doctor, incorporating the old staff grade and associate specialist grades, but also potentially allowing progression to admission to the specialist register, has made relationships more complicated. These doctors generally have not progressed far enough in training to be admitted to the specialist register and still work under the supervision of a consultant who is on the specialist register and who retains a degree of responsibility for the clinical quality of their work. Consultants who have worked with high-quality staff grade and associate specialist colleagues will appreciate that a 'light touch' supervisory relationship can be very success-ful. However, some doctors in this grade expect to work too independently and may resent supervision. Issues of quality and clinical responsibility will have to be clearly negotiated and understood if this grade is to multiply (as envisaged by some NHS employers).

EXERCISE 2.2

Delegation in clinical practice: Before delegating a piece of work to a junior colleague, consultants need to consider the junior's competencies and what level of delegation is appropriate. They also need to be explicit about the level of delegation. For the task of reviewing a patient referred from a general practitioner or hospital consultant, three possible levels of delegation are described below:

1   'See the patient, make notes and discuss with me and see the patient together before deciding on and recording a management plan'.
2   'See the patient, make notes, decide on and record a provisional diagnosis and management plan. Discuss with me (and see the patient together and/or make modifications to the plan if necessary) before it is implemented'.
3   'See the patient, make notes, decide on and record a management plan. Only discuss with me immediately if you are uncertain or perceive a possible problem. Otherwise present the case briefly in routine clinical supervision'.

You may wish to modify these levels. When you are satisfied with them, consider what level(s) of delegation are appropriate to the doctors who work under your supervision as trainees or in 'staff' positions. Are you explicit about the level of delegation when you ask a doctor under your supervision to undertake an assessment or other clinical task? (What about delegation of management or administrative tasks to assistants or clerical staff? How do these principles apply in that situation?)

Relationships with medical 'peers'

Here we are of course not talking about relationships with colleagues (in the UK) who have been elevated to the House of Lords but with colleagues at an equivalent 'level' in their careers. When we are in training our peers are our colleagues at the same stage in their training. When we become consultants or principals in general practice, other consultants and general practitioners are our peers. Because of the historical idea that once we are ready for 'independent' practice (on the specialist or GP register in modern parlance) we are all 'master craftsmen', the relationships between doctors in management and their consultant/principal colleagues (which will be discussed later) can also be viewed as peer relationships even though they may contain a supervisory element.

Medical peer relationships are important, particularly for those in the consultant or equivalent grades. 'Independent practice' is an old-fashioned notion. 'Interdependence' better describes the modern situation where technical advances have made it necessary that we trust and work closely with colleagues in other specialist areas. We all value highly a radiologist, haematologist or chemical pathologist who provides timely and concise reports and advice on unusual findings, or specialist colleagues who advise on a condition that may be commonplace to them but appears complicated and unusual to us!

High-quality relationships are essential between general practitioners and specialists in specialties dealing with chronic illnesses in the community rather than 'one-off' interventions in hospital. Both consultants and GPs need to work to develop and sustain such relationships. One way of doing this for consultants is by going out and meeting GPs in local practices to seek their views on service provision and to seek opportunities for mutual learning. A more formal but even more important way of working together is by developing 'shared care' protocols for common diseases and disorders. Finally, perhaps the most important way of working together is working together in the care of individual patients. This personal collaboration has been discounted with the development of ever-more fragmented patterns of care but it is important for patients and for doctors.

Within a specialty, peer groups can, through clinical audit, second opinions and confidential discussion of case management, provide a valuable space to reflect on and refine practice. This kind of case-based discussion is likely to become an increasingly important part of development for doctors in training and of appraisal for consultants. In any case, we would advocate consultants (and general practitioners) finding more time to discuss 'difficult cases' with their colleagues in addition to more structured clinical audit projects. Sustained effort is needed to maintain cooperative relationships. Competition of a friendly nature can be beneficial but hostile competition makes for an unhappy workplace.

Relationships between doctors in management and other doctors

The exercise of power is a delicate matter. The old 'merit award' system in the British NHS used to give senior colleagues in hospital specialties an unspecified power in deciding who was 'meritorious' (and therefore who got significant supplements to their salaries). Now, the 'Clinical Excellence Award' system is more locally controlled (some would say more democratic, certainly more bureaucratic). This local control puts significant 'levers' into the hands of doctors in management positions, especially medical directors. (Incidentally, the language of 'levers', like the language of 'driving' change, is, in the view of the authors, disrespectful and can be counterproductive.) These 'levers' should not be abused since most people are motivated best by an environment that encourages an appropriate degree of autonomy, where there is a sharing of vision and values and where they have an opportunity to achieve. Fear and greed are poor motivators. We generally get the best out of people when we respect their abilities and (in the words of Chief Medical Officer Liam Donaldson, when clinical governance was introduced) when we strive to 'create an environment in which clinical excellence can flourish'.[6]

But we are getting ahead of ourselves. Consultant practice in the UK NHS has tended to be a very autonomous affair. In the heyday of the asylums there had been doctors in charge ('medical superintendents'); but until the 1990s the only doctors in formal management positions tended to be public health physicians with roles as area, district or regional medical officers. Consultants and GPs still tended to regard themselves as independent practitioners, answerable only to the GMC. With the introduction of NHS trusts, medical management became more formal. Every trust was required to have a medical director with board-level responsibilities. In hospital trusts they were often supported by consultant 'clinical directors' in specialties or clusters of specialties. Some mental health trusts adopted a similar structure. Others had 'associate medical directors' divided by specialty or, sometimes, by geographical area or other area of responsibility (e.g. research and development or education).

The creation of primary care trusts (PCTs) also increased the management positions filled by GPs. No doubt the move to primary care consortia for commissioning will increase the management involvement of some GPs (and if it works properly, of consultant doctors in provider organisations).

In parallel with these organisational changes came ideas of the need to formalise continuing professional development. The idea that the organisation and its CEO were responsible not just for financial and corporate governance but also for the overall quality of clinical services soon followed.[6]

This and other pressures led to a demand for job planning, appraisal and eventually revalidation, recertification and relicensing of consultants and GPs. There is nothing wrong with these rather bureaucratic responses to the need to ensure quality except that (by themselves) they do not work and they tend to downgrade the value of personal autonomy (or self-control!). However, even though they can be very time consuming, they do help in some ways. Good doctors working in good organisations have always kept up to date with their skills and with the evidence base in their areas of practice. Good doctors in poor organisations have often found it hard to find the time (and funding) for these activities. Now that it is mandated from the top down, healthcare organisations find it hard to refuse time and money for appropriate continuing professional development.

To return to the point that by themselves bureaucratic measures do not work, let us consider an example from another field. There are recurrent scandals about childcare, usually focusing on the failure of social workers and healthcare workers to detect abuse and act appropriately. Again the response tends to be bureaucratic, with enquiries that produce long lists of recommendations. Inspectorates 'ensure' the recommendations are followed, at least on paper. The culture tends to be one of fear, restricted autonomy, alienation and form-filling. Often departments are under-resourced for the work they are expected to do and even if they have resources the 'atmosphere' makes it hard to attract good staff. Good leadership and management is about changing this atmosphere; about changing the culture from high blame, top-down command and control to one where professionals exercise their skills with an appropriate degree of autonomy while working with a shared purpose and understanding. This attracts people to work in the organisation and to take responsibility. It is this kind of culture change that makes the real difference and that requires good leadership if it is to be developed and sustained.

Doctors in management have many responsibilities but those that give most opportunity for creating a positive culture among medical staff are roles in the appraisal and job planning cycle and roles in managing performance.

APPRAISAL AND JOB PLANNING

Appraisal is a complicated affair. The Department of Health website states that 'the primary aim of NHS appraisal is to identify personal and professional development needs . . .' Others see appraisal as a tool for performance management or (in education) as a way of helping a student assess their own progress ('formative assessment' quite separate from any process to assess achievement of required standards, known as 'summative assessment' (*see* Box 2.4).

BOX 2.4 Different meanings of appraisal

- In education: a process whereby students are encouraged to review their progress with their supervisor. Kept separate from *summative assessment.*
- In business: part of the performance management cycle where managers ensure supervisees are performing well in accordance with objectives. May link to bonuses!
- In the NHS, for doctors: both of these and more!

At the moment the format of annual appraisals for doctors is heavily specified by the Department of Health. There are four mandatory forms and an additional two, one of which tends to repeat the fourth form and is intended as a link between appraisal and the job-planning process and the other, a detailed record, reserved for times when there is dispute. This is not the place to go into detail about the forms, which may well change anyway as revalidation, recertification and relicensing are introduced. In addition the GMC is requiring that all doctors have approved feedback from clinicians, managers and patients (modelled on so-called '360 degree appraisal'). Here we do not want to go into details about Department of Health or GMC requirements. We want instead to discuss how medical managers can:

➤ make appraisal as beneficial as possible
➤ encourage a culture of personal development
➤ encourage personal responsibility and accountability
➤ ensure the whole process (including job-planning) be used to facilitate alignment between the goals of the organisation and the goals of the individual.

The alternative is 'going through the motions' in a lifeless (and unpleasant) process of form-filling to satisfy the bureaucracy.

A CULTURAL CHANGE?

Can the appraisal–job-planning–continuing professional development cycle be used to effect and/or maintain a change in culture away from the high-blame bureaucratic style towards a low-blame (not no blame!) partnership or team approach? We believe it can, despite the extra pressures introduced by the five-year revalidation, recertification and relicensing cycle. Doctors are generally highly motivated to help other people. If we set up the appraisal and job-planning process so that it strengthens this motivation we will do better than if we set up a performance management culture where the doctor is seen as a reluctant performer. Annual appraisal gives people a great opportunity to reflect on the year looking at:

➤ clinical and other work
➤ continuing professional development
➤ relationships with patients
➤ relationships with colleagues
➤ relationships with managers
➤ mismatch between organisational expectations and resources.

Coupled with job planning it also gives a vital opportunity to look at personal and organisational goals for the next year and ensure that they are reasonably aligned. The appraiser should be willing to listen to the person being appraised, to ask questions designed to elicit self-awareness in the appraisee, to provide accurate feedback (including praise and, where necessary, constructive criticism). Above all, appraisal and job planning should be an opportunity for the person being appraised to reflect on the last year and plan for the next. It could partly be seen as an exercise in supporting and developing emotional intelligence! So-called 360 degree appraisal gives the appraisee feedback from a variety of colleagues (doctors, nurses, secretaries, other healthcare professionals, GPs, voluntary sector, patients and carers) and is likely to be a required part of revalidation. Feedback from 360 degree appraisal needs to be managed carefully, to avoid unwanted negative side effects, and the 360 degree appraisal can feed into the annual appraisal. The Royal College of Psychiatrists is also proposing to introduce case-based discussions into the appraisal process at a rate of two per annum (10 over a five-year revalidation cycle).

MANAGING PERFORMANCE

Senior doctors generally manage their own performance. The job-planning interview gives them and their medical manager an opportunity to review this against agreed goals and standards. If these have not been attained it is often for systemic reasons. Have there been obstacles that could not be overcome? Have sufficient resources been made available to make the goal realistic? If the goal is still relevant, what can be done to make it more attainable in the coming year? This is a two-sided bargain and it is important that both sides work hard to realise agreed goals. Only where doctors are failing to meet objectives despite adequate support from the organisation should the medical manager need to consider how the doctor needs to change so that performance can be improved.

It seems likely that, as re-validation is introduced, medical directors will become 'responsible officers' and will need to satisfy themselves that appraisals over the five-year cycle have met the required standards.

Under-performance

The risk of under-performance is minimised if the conditions in the workplace are good, with:
> adequate support
> reasonable workload
> good relationships
> shared purpose
> clarity about responsibilities
> an appropriate degree of autonomy
> an opportunity to exercise skills.

However, it can still occur, for a variety of reasons. The National Clinical Assessment Service (NCAS) website provides a comprehensive guide to this area in the form of a 'toolkit'.[7] NCAS will also provide direct help and guidance to medical managers dealing with these issues. An NCAS review of cases they have helped with categorises problems as arising from health, behavioural issues or clinical capability. Over a two-year period, taking concerns in combination, there were slightly more concerns about behaviour (67%) than clinical capability (61%); 29% of cases were about behaviour alone and 20% involved a practitioner health problem of some sort.

When an issue concerning the performance of a colleague comes to a medical manager, they need first to determine who the appropriate person is to deal with it. All NHS organisations have carefully thought out and negotiated policies and procedures that have to be followed. The principles that underpin these are generally similar.
> Protect patients from risk.
> Seek advice from human resources managers and (if appropriate) NCAS or (for trainees) the relevant deanery authorities.
> Find out the facts using agreed procedures.
> Decide (in consultation) whether the matter can be dealt with informally.
> If the matter needs to be dealt with formally decide (in consultation with human resources and appropriate authorities) which procedures

(health/capability/conduct) are appropriate and follow them fairly and swiftly.

In cases where fitness to practise is affected, it is necessary to inform the GMC. Again, NCAS, local procedures and other sources of advice will help in making decisions.

The NCAS website[7] and dedicated books[8] provide help in detail beyond the scope of this book.

RELATIONSHIPS WITH MANAGERS

Managers in health and social care are a diverse group. They are often drawn from the ranks of the clinical professions into general management roles. The advantages this brings are considerable. Hopefully, they understand some of the complexities of real-life clinical care and hopefully they still have some of the patient-centred ethos that characterises the clinical professions at their best. Increasingly however, general managers, human resources managers and other specialists are drawn from the graduate population through the NHS management training scheme. Their basic degree will be in business studies or a related discipline and they will often be studying for a diploma or master's degree in health service management and leadership. Clearly people coming through this route will have more initial training in management and may well have competencies and skills that the manager coming through the clinical route traditionally acquired over time through practice. They may, in their training, be exposed to clinical situations as they help manage projects on waiting lists, turnover and so on, but they will have to work harder than managers who have come from clinical backgrounds to gain genuine empathy for the reality of complex and often unpredictable clinical work.

The distinctions between administration, management and leadership are useful here (*see* Chapter 1). Remember, good administration means doing routine tasks well, good management involves making things happen even when the environment is complex and good leadership means helping a group or organisation find its direction *and* drawing the best out of people to serve a common purpose. At a junior level, managers may be concerned with a mixture of administrative, leadership, management and clinical tasks (for example, the ward manager). At an intermediate level (except in medicine) the clinical work disappears and administration and management predominate. This is the level at which non-clinical graduate managers enter. At more senior levels still, administrative and managerial skills remain important foundations but leadership ability becomes increasingly important. Senior managers will have specialist knowledge, skills and competencies, for example in finance or human resources. Medical directors, directors of nursing and clinical directors retain strong links to their professions of origin.

With such a diverse group there can be few generalisations. Working relationships must be based on general principles. What makes effective relationships at work? You will remember the list from the previous chapter:

➤ mutual respect
➤ shared vision (and mission)
➤ shared values
➤ clear definitions of roles and responsibilities
➤ flexibility (within limits)
➤ integrity.

Senior managers need these principles as much as anybody else. Indeed, they need to model them for the whole organisation.

At board level, it is important for people to know enough of each other's functions to exercise corporate responsibility. This does not mean that the medical director needs to know as much about accounting as the finance director or as much about personnel management as the human resources director. However he or she needs to know enough to contribute responsibly to decision-making and enough to know when to ask for help from fellow directors in operational decisions.

RELATIONSHIPS WITH SERVICE USERS

Medical managers will have been accustomed to relating to patients as service users. Now they will have to relate to them in other roles, too. They will have to relate to them as representatives on various decision-making bodies, as colleagues in managing various projects and occasionally as complainants or even as litigants. The last two roles demand a degree of reserve and caution that may not come naturally to the clinician in these informal days!

Service-user representatives, patients and carers will often form natural alliances with clinical managers. They sometimes carry more influence with decision-makers than clinicians so that making sure they are well informed and seeking their views and their support becomes an important part of securing improvements in the service.

As complainants, service users deserve to be treated with respect and frankness. If an informal complaint is dealt with respectfully *and* effectively it will often not develop into a formal complaint. The legal system in the UK is (with the exception of coroners' courts) 'adversarial'. Unfortunately complaints can develop into litigation and those dealing with complaints often feel limited by considerations of what will happen if litigation follows. This is another reason for dealing with complaints at an early, informal stage whenever possible. Clinicians need to be aware if patients or relatives are dissatisfied with the service they are receiving and to take reasonable steps to deal with any concerns. Martin Luther King once said 'violence is the voice of the unheard'. Certainly the formal complaint is often the result of people feeling that their concerns have not been properly 'heard' and dealt with.

Senior medical managers should do all they can to ensure that clinical staff are sensitive to patients' and relatives' concerns and are competent to deal with them before they develop into complaints. This is an important aspect of leadership. When a formal complaint does arise, it is dealt with by a formal process, which rarely leaves all parties feeling that they have been fairly treated. Medical managers will have various roles in this process. The medical director will see the results of investigations following complaints that involve doctors and may help in the drafting of the formal response that the chief executive sends to the complainant. Another important role for the medical manager is to make sure that doctors who are complained against receive appropriate support throughout the process of handling the complaint. Additionally, the manager may need to arrange further training or support arising from the outcome of the complaint. Rarely disciplinary action against doctors may follow, and the medical director will have to make a decision about this. For this reason, senior medical managers need to remain unprejudiced.

People who need health services ('patients' or potential patients!) are the reason for the existence of health services, clinicians and medical managers. Being 'patient-centred' is the common ground on which managers and clinicians can and should come together. Unfortunately, the strong central direction of modern health services has caused some people working in the service to be more concerned with reaching 'targets' than with the real needs of patients. Of course if the targets were perfectly patient-centred this would not cause any conflict. Unfortunately, central targets can sometimes be difficult to adapt to local circumstances and that is one of the many challenges facing medical managers. After the change of government in the UK in 2010 there is some indication that central targets in England are being reduced. However, a massive change is envisaged in commissioning arrangements with a much more competitive environment for providers. This pressure to further commercialise the NHS will be accompanied by a relative reduction in investment and will generate its own distractions from patient-centred care. The important thing, in the face of all political and managerial fashions and imperatives, is to keep the needs of service users central and to develop the alliance between patients and the clinical professions that ultimately serve *them*, not the organisation.

RELATIONSHIPS, RELATIONSHIPS, RELATIONSHIPS

In the end, given adequate clinical and managerial competency in the more technical areas, the ability to develop and sustain high-quality relationships between doctors, managers, other professionals and workers and patients remains a vital foundation for good practice and good management.

REFERENCES

1 Goleman S. *Emotional Intelligence and Working with Emotional Intelligence.* London: Bloomsbury Publishing; 2004.
2 Morgan G. *Images of Organization.* London: Sage Publications; 2006.
3 Solomon C. Transactional analysis theory: the basics. *Transactional Anal J.* 2003; **33**: 15–22.
4 Rath B, Conchie T. *Strengths Based Leadership.* Washington: Gallup Press; 2009.
5 Covey S. *The 7 Habits of Highly Effective People.* London: Simon and Schuster; 2004.
6 Department of Health. *Clinical Governance: moving from rhetoric to reality.* London: Department of Health; 1998.
7 National Clinical Assessment Service (NCAS). Available online at: www. ncas.npsa.nhs.uk/ (accessed 1 January 2011).
8 Cox J, King J, Hutchinson A, *et al. Understanding Doctors' Performance.* Oxford: Radcliffe Publishing; 2005.

CHAPTER 3

Understanding your organisation

Health services are often complex organisations that are difficult to understand. The British NHS is the organisation that the authors are most familiar with and it is no exception! In fact, since political devolution of control of health services to Wales and Scotland, different parts of the UK health service have developed in different ways, so that one can no longer refer to the NHS as a whole.

There are many different tools for understanding organisations and a brief, practical text like this cannot aim to be comprehensive. Instead, we will follow a pragmatic approach with a brief historical account of the NHS followed by two different perspectives taken from the work of Gareth Morgan[1] and Charles Handy.[2] Although the context is British, the influences on healthcare systems are now global and so the same principles can be applied to understanding any health system:

➤ historical development
➤ use of metaphors to enhance understanding
➤ especially understanding the different cultures within the organisation and within which the organisation functions.

A BRIEF HISTORY OF THE NHS

The British NHS came into being in 1948, after the Second World War. It was essentially shaped on mechanistic or bureaucratic lines with a top-down 'command and control' structure. Control was partly by central government through regional boards, partly by local executive committees (general practitioners, opticians, dentists and pharmacies) and partly by local government (public health and ambulance services). Teaching hospitals retained a degree of independence with their own boards of governors. The centralised structure modelled on the Emergency Medical Service which had performed well in the face of the disruption and casualties caused by the bombing of cities during the Second World War. There were incremental changes over many years. Then, in the 1990s, under the influence of economic theorists from Europe and the USA, there was a fundamental change with the introduction of a market-oriented system with a purchaser–provider split, at least at the secondary care level. A service ethos was partly replaced by a market ethos, where organisations competed for customers (patients) via their GPs and where financial efficiency was the bottom line. After a brief respite, the process of introducing market forces continued in the form of 'world class commissioning' and primary care trusts (PCTs) that purchased health services from provider organisations and exercised a measure of control over primary care providers, too.

In England, commissioners were helped in their tasks by various organisations like the National Mental Health Development Unit and the National Institute for Health and Clinical Excellence (NICE), which set standards and approved treatments for NHS use at the (English) national level, with different arrangements in different parts of the UK. The tension between the old 'service model' and the new 'commissioner–provider' model was high in the area of service design. The old system tended to rely on the expertise of local clinicians, especially consultants. The new system relied on evidence abstracted at a higher level through organisations like NICE. There was a potential for more superficial uniformity but perhaps at the expense of innovation and inspired clinical leadership.

In an attempt to ensure that standards were maintained there were inspectorates (the Care Quality Commission, in its latest incarnation) and (for 'foundation trusts' and mainly for financial governance matters) Monitor. The inadequacy of these arrangements was nicely demonstrated in 2009 when the Mid Staffordshire NHS Foundation Trust, in its anxiety to achieve foundation status, concentrated on financial savings and not on a marked excess mortality, possibly at least in part due to some of the cuts. A subsequent investigation by the Healthcare Commission (the predecessor to the Care Quality Commission) found, among other failings, that the trust had shed too many clinical staff in an effort to balance the books. From the narrow point of view of Monitor, they succeeded, being granted foundation status just before the Healthcare Commission commenced its inquiry. Nor did the Healthcare Commission come out of the episode covered in glory. The excess mortality was first picked up by a semi-independent public health monitoring body called 'Dr Foster' (www.drfosterintelligence.co.uk/), not by the commission.

Strategic health authorities at regional level tried to hold it all together and provided support to the PCTs and related commissioner organisations. The detailed situation varied from year to year but the basic division was and still is into commissioning bodies and provider organisations with separate standard setting and inspecting bodies.

According to the 2008/9 staff census figures from the NHS Information Centre, the number of managers in the NHS has risen to 39 900 – a 9.4% increase. Managers now outnumbered consultants by 5 000 and midwives by 15 000. Although the NHS Confederation defended this increase, other observers were beginning to ask whether the increasing transaction and inspection costs associated with the commissioner–provider split were justified. This was especially pertinent in a period when the financial markets had collapsed, suggesting that even regulated markets have their limitations and that greed may not be the best motivating factor for the common good.

The change of government in 2010 was preceded by a promise of no more radical changes in the NHS and followed by the most radical changes yet! The White Paper presented in the middle of 2010[3] proposed a much more open health market with GP (primary care) consortia as the purchasers and a plurality of providers. Despite the massive costs of reorganisation and the likelihood that many managers will simply switch to work for new organisations, the proposals (combined with measures introduced by the previous government) will allegedly save £20 billion over four years and be associated with a 45% cut in management costs. This will be 're-invested' in front-line services. Thus, if the savings are not made it will be front-line services that will suffer. Interestingly, public health will be partly returned to local authority control. There will certainly be many challenges facing medical managers as they try to sustain and develop services in the face of yet more politically motivated change.

At the time of writing it is too early to predict all the effects of the proposed reorganisation but some of the possible implications are briefly outlined in Box 3.1. Clearly these changes and managing the transition to the new system will demand a great deal of management skill and flexibility from doctors in both primary and secondary care organisations.

BOX 3.1 Some implications of further reorganisation

Competition and commercialisation: Monitor (*see* p. 38) will have a new duty to promote competition and choice will be extended to 'any willing provider'. There is a risk of commercial organisations 'cherry picking' the easy-to-provide and profitable services leaving foundation trusts to deal with the difficult and costly. However foundation trusts themselves will become much more commercially oriented so that conditions that are persistent and difficult to manage may be relatively neglected.

Secondary care provision: Secondary care NHS organisations will become or become part of foundation trusts or social enterprises. NHS staff will also be encouraged to create employee-led social enterprises. This model has yet to be fully worked out but has the merit of employees being serious stakeholders in the organisation and perhaps having more influence on its direction.

Commissioning consortia: Details are yet to emerge but consortia will need to be of sufficient size to fulfil many of the functions currently filled by PCTs. With the ever-continuing development of medicine, services will continue to be delivered in the community and through the primary care team whenever possible. This may lead to conflict of interest and loss of quality in services for vulnerable groups who need a high level of expertise but who are best managed in the community (for example people with long-standing mental health problems).

When we examine the flux and transformation metaphors of organisation later in this chapter, the relevance of the political and economic context may be evident.

METAPHORS AS A FRAMEWORK FOR UNDERSTANDING

The task for the medical manager is first of all to understand his or her own service, how this fits into the organisation to which it belongs, and then to understand how the organisation fits into the wider healthcare system. We use many concepts in trying to understand organisations but one of the most powerful is metaphor. Gareth Morgan discusses eight powerful metaphors that help us to understand organisations (*see* Box 3.2).[1]

BOX 3.2 Morgan's metaphors of organisations

- Organisations as machines.
- Organisations as organisms.
- Organisations as brains: learning and self-organisation.
- Organisations as cultures: creating social reality.
- Organisations as political systems: interests, conflicts and power.

- Organisations as psychic prisons.
- Organisation as flux and transformation.
- Organisations as instruments of domination.

All these metaphors can help us to understand an organisation (and they all have limitations). Good doctor–managers will seek to take a number of different points of view as they grapple with an organisational problem. Other metaphors will occur, too, such as organisational diagnosis and treatment! There is no space here to explore all the metaphors and too many different perspectives can be confusing. We have selected two of the most pertinent to modern health services to discuss in more detail:

1   Organisations as cultures.
2   Organisations as flux and change.

This is not arbitrary. One of the authors found the first of these particularly useful when he first moved into medical management because it helped him see that different parts of the NHS have different cultures, implying different modes of operation, motivators, success criteria and time scales. The second is chosen because it is the one most doctors instantly recognise as relevant to ever-changing modern health services.

Organisational culture

The idea of management cultures first came to prominence following the phenomenal success of Japanese industry after the Second World War. Academics who studied management realised that there were cultural factors at work. Another, more topical, example is the 'bonus culture' in banks that preceded the financial crash of 2008. In this case it is possible to make a case that traces the diffusion of American child-rearing practice first into American commercial culture and then into the global marketplace. The idea is very simple. Wanted behaviour should be rewarded, preferably with tangible rewards. So, the theorist might argue, the practice of giving children sweets for being good led to the practice of giving fund managers bonuses for doing their job 'well' (i.e. securing short-term profits). Fuelled by greed, this led to ever-more complex schemes for 'making money' and then to disaster! Culture can be very powerful.

Charles Handy is sometimes described as the only 'home grown' British 'management guru'. (In fact he was born in Ireland.) Indeed the term 'management guru' was allegedly coined by a journalist to describe him. Writing at the end of the twentieth century,[2] he described four dominant cultures in modern organisations. He identified each with a god from Greek mythology (reflecting his own classical education). His scheme undoubtedly oversimplifies but is still incredibly helpful in understanding why different bits of the organisation behave in different ways. Handy also proposed a theory of 'cultural propriety' that suggests that all the cultures are equally valid but that each has its place.

Table 3.1 lists some of the attributes of the four cultures described by Handy.

TABLE 3.1 Charles Handy's dominant cultures of organisations[2]

'God' and culture	Attributes	Best suited to:	Control and influence
Zeus: the 'club' culture	Based on knowing (the top) people, makes speedy, intuitive decisions.	Small *entrepreneurial* (often family) businesses. Also found at senior levels in politics!	Personal praise or punishment from the 'boss'. *Who* you know is more important than *what* you know.
Apollo: the 'role' culture	Related to the 'machine' metaphor, essentially sees people according to their roles, as replaceable parts in the organisation.	Routine tasks where change is minimal and unexpected variation unusual; surprisingly common in the NHS given the amount and pace of change.	Impersonal exercise of economic and political power to enforce standards and procedures. Room size, desk size, car size = 'status'.
Athena: the 'task' culture	Focus on the continual and successful definition and solution of problems.	Team working to solve problems where complexity and variety are common. A common culture for the clinician. May waste time/resources in routine settings.	Personal commitment to the task, rewarded by success. Team members valued for their competencies rather than who they know or their role 'labels'.
Dionysus: the 'existential' or 'craft' culture	The organisation is there to enable Dionysians to achieve their purpose.	Situations where *individual* talents or skills are most important. Also found in clinical practice.	Enjoyment intrinsic to the exercise of skills (which may include meeting the needs of others).

Handy's book includes a questionnaire for individuals to look at their own cultural preferences and those of their organisations.

EXERCISE 3.1

Consider your own organisation. How does it work at various levels? If you work in a clinical team, does the team subdivide to tackle the tasks around the individual needs of patients or are you more a collection of individualists, each exercising their own skills in the service of patients but without much coordination? Do different disciplines in the team work according to different models? What about the immediate organisation you work for? How important is the enforcement of standards and procedures? Do conflicts arise between different cultures? How much scope is there for team working? Are people expected to enjoy their work? How does your organisation compare with the wider health service in terms of its dominant 'gods'? How do your own cultural expectations mesh with those of the organisation?

Consider how appropriate different cultures are for different tasks. How do Athenans or Dionysians feel in an Appolonian organisation? What are the vices and virtues of each culture? If you really want to get a grip on this have a look at the book *The Gods of Management* and try the questionnaire in the chapter on 'the gods at work'.[2]

Doctors working in the health service often see themselves as Athenans or Dionysians working in organisations that are still predominantly Appolonian. This causes tension. Figure 3.1 illustrates the proposed new management structure of the NHS from two different perspectives; the first (Figure 3.1a) is a 'top-down' organisation chart, modified slightly from *Equity and Excellence*[3]; the second (Figure 3.1b) is a patient-centred team culture that usually works at the clinical level. Both these illustrations have validity. The first is keener in terms of issues of responsibility and accountability. The second perspective accords with 'messy reality'.

Figure 3.1b illustrates how clinicians of all disciplines work within their provider organisations and in collaboration with a wider network of other providers to help people resolve their health problems. The complexity (and cost) of interventions may vary from the prescription of an antibiotic to treat an uncomplicated bacterial infection in primary care to the coordinated provision of care and treatment for people with enduring and disabling physical and mental illness. The focus is on bringing together the right resources to efficiently meet patients' needs. Clinicians may not see much of the health-care system beyond the parts that are needed for 'their' patients. Although

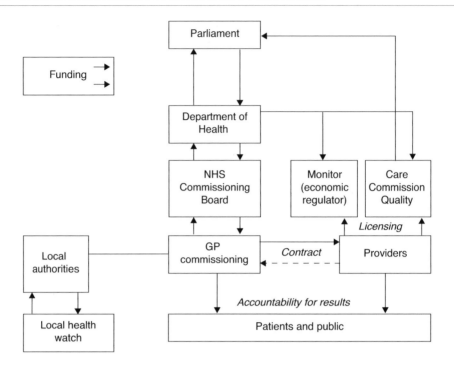

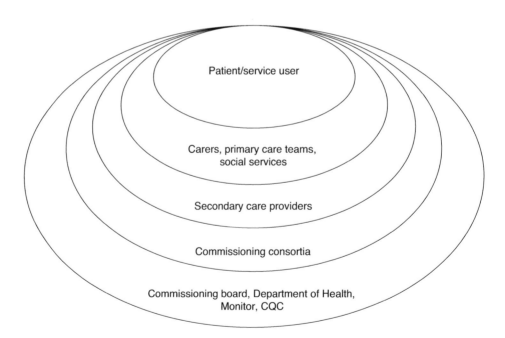

FIGURE 3.1 (a) The English NHS as a (top-down) role culture. (b) The English NHS as a (patient-centred) team culture

sometimes acting as individuals, they are part of an essentially 'team' culture.

However, doctors in management need to have a wider appreciation of the culture(s) of the health service. Handy does not suggest that one culture is 'better' than another. He speaks of 'cultural appropriateness'. Thus a role culture may be good at regular, repetitive tasks such as paying salaries, but hopeless at dealing with the complexities of a real-life clinical emergency where the team culture is generally most appropriate. Problems arise when the different cultures do not know their place in the wider scheme of things. One of the tasks for a medical manager is to ensure that cultural appropriateness is not violated. Another task is to understand the different cultures and their different languages ('jargon') so as to be able to adequately represent one to the other without misunderstanding.

Another way at looking at cultures in healthcare is to examine the development of health services in the UK in the last century. Before the NHS there was a market culture, supplemented by various forms of insurance and the individual charitable donation of time to 'the poor' by some doctors and

TABLE 3.2 Evolution and development of dominant cultures in health services

Culture	Market	Service	Commissioner–Provider	Consumer
Who 'knows' best?	Buyer.	Provider.	Commissioner.	Service user.
Who disposes of resources?	Buyer.	Provider.	Commissioner.	Service user limited by commissioner.
Who is in charge?	Buyer.	Provider.	Commissioner.	Service user (in theory!).
Some advantages:	Good for those with lots of money.	Providers *do* know more. Demands altruism in workers to work well.	Interests of different stakeholders considered.	Service user is 'empowered'.
Some disadvantages:	Bad for those who are poor.	'Producer capture' – run in interest of workers not users.	Costly extra layers of management. Duplication of supporting functions.	Costly extra layers of management. Service user empowerment may be illusory.

organisations. The early NHS was predominantly a top-down organisation with strong elements of role culture but with clinicians relatively free to function independently. We have called this a 'service culture'. Then, under the influence of economic and political theorists, the internal market was introduced, here described as the 'commissioner–provider' culture. This was designed to remedy the so-called 'producer capture' where the 'workers' of public service industries were (somewhat insultingly) seen as running the business for their own benefit. Gains in efficiency were also predicted (though the long-term efficiency of markets must now be in some doubt). Finally, running alongside this evolution, we have the wider phenomenon of the consumer culture. Table 3.2 gives a simplified account of the characteristics of these different cultures. As the English NHS evolves, the consumer model, as presented here, is essentially a market model with service commissioners acting as moderators and purchasers of service on behalf of consumers.

Organisations as flux and transformation

Since the 1990s the NHS has been in a state of continuous flux and change. The ideas ('logics of change') that Morgan uses to give insight into this metaphor are as follows.

➤ Autopoiesis: a new way at looking at organisational relationships with their environment.
➤ Chaos and complexity theory: how ordered patterns can emerge from spontaneous self-organisation.
➤ Cybernetics: exploring the way change is 'enfolded' in circular relations.
➤ The dialectic dimension: change as a function of tensions between opposites.

Autopoiesis

The conventional logic of systems theory sees the organisation as a system within an environment to which it needs to respond. It is helpful and is seen in various techniques, including the following.

➤ 'STEP' analysis, where an organisation systematically looks at the Social, Technical, Economic and Political factors in the environment that need to be considered in planning its business.
➤ 'SWOT' analysis, where the Strengths, Weaknesses, Opportunities and Threats to an organisation seen as an organism reacting to an outside environment are explored (*see* Chapter 6 for more details).

Autopoiesis (another biologically derived metaphor) suggests that organisations are essentially self-referential. An organisation's interaction with the 'environment' is really a reflection and part of its own organisation. It interacts with the environment in a way that favours its own survival and 'self-production'. All parts of the wider system (around which it is impossible to draw realistic boundaries) influence other parts in a reflexive and mutually dependent way. Morgan gives the biological example of the honeybee. Bees are linked with botanical, agricultural, animal, human and social systems. Eliminate the bee and we all go hungry! Each element of a well-functioning system combines the maintenance of itself with the maintenance of other parts of the system. Thus the commissioners and different providers have their niches and are not necessarily in a race for 'survival of the fittest' as suggested by more simplistic analyses. 'Egocentric' organisations tend to ignore or undervalue this systemic wisdom. The autopoietic metaphor also helps explain why organisations providing health services tend to evolve with the body politic. It explains the shift from service to market philosophies as socialism has become nearly as unpopular on this side of the Atlantic as in the USA. The recent collapse of the financial markets from greed and over-complexity may also bring more general societal changes, which will be reflected in healthcare systems (*see* next section).

Chaos, complexity and cybernetics

Chaos theory and complexity theory provide further insight into how organisations behave in real life. Complex organisations are characterised by multiple systems of interaction that are at once ordered and chaotic. Random events can produce massive reverberations in the system with consequent chaos. Nevertheless order reasserts itself. A good example would be the global economic crisis of 2008–09. Here the effects of sub-prime mortgages in the USA destabilised a system that had been made overcomplicated by traders seeking to maximise their own bonuses. Eventually order will reassert itself. Whether it will be the 'old order' of under-regulated global market capitalism, or whether a more regulated order will supervene, or whether some completely new approach will prove most attractive remains (at the time of writing) to be seen.

Medical managers often have to deal with unexpected events that appear 'random' in their timing if not in their actual occurrence. These include doctors falling ill or misbehaving, complaints, politically motivated changes in the organisation of the service, epidemics and many other events. Just as the behaviour of a flock of birds or a shoal of fish can be modelled on a computer by a few simple rules, so we can bring ourselves through the apparent chaos and complexity of the healthcare system by holding on to a few simple principles of 'good management practice'.

EXERCISE 3.2

> Consider some of the difficult management situations you have faced. Write a brief account of what happened. What were the learning points? What principles did you use to guide you through the situation? What new principles (if any) did you learn? How do these principles relate to your core values as a doctor? (Look at the GMC guidance if it helps.) Do you have the same or different core values as a manager?

Dialectics

This is essentially a philosophical (and political) theory stating that change emerges out of a *synthesis* between a *thesis* and an *antithesis*. In politics the tension between opposing theories and viewpoints produces an emergent new order. The relationship between this and chaos/complexity theory is obvious.

PRACTICAL APPLICATIONS

In the midst of complexity we need to:
- rethink what we mean by organisations and how they are 'controlled'
- learn the art of managing and changing contexts
- learn how to use small changes to achieve large effects
- live with continual transformation and emergent order
- be open to new ideas.

(Adapted from Morgan)[1]

Changing contexts

A good example of an attempt to manage by changing contexts was the introduction of clinical governance into the NHS. Corporate governance and financial probity were early targets in the formation of NHS trusts. Then the concept of *clinical governance* was introduced 'to create an environment in which clinical excellence will flourish'. The idea was to change the context so that clinical excellence was as important to the boards of NHS trusts as was financial probity. (The recent example of the Mid Staffordshire NHS Foundation Trust, cited above, suggests the message may not have been well received in all areas.) A good part of health service management can be seen as creating a reasonably stable environment for clinicians of all disciplines to do their jobs. Within this metaphor, *the fundamental role of managers is to create contexts in which appropriate forms of self-organisation can occur.* Morgan actually cites the organisation of a hospital emergency department as an example where managers need to provide a stable and resilient context within which clinicians of all disciplines can self-organise to meet a variety of very different and sometimes complex challenges.

Small changes to achieve large effects

When a system resists change, for example the move from hospital-dominated 'clinics' to community assessment and treatment in psychiatry, one effective small change can be to harness the enthusiasm of a small group to run a successful 'pilot'. By demonstrating that different ways of working are possible this can pave the way for larger-scale changes. However, one should never underestimate the power of old patterns of working to reassert themselves. In the authors' own specialty of old-age psychiatry, the pattern of home assessment by senior medical staff was an important shift from the outpatient model of assessment. However, as teams and 'new ways of working' have developed, much of the community assessment is carried out by non-medical members of the team with doctors (perhaps appropriately) partly retreating to conduct their assessments in clinic settings (which have advantages and disadvantages).

EXERCISE 3.3

Look at the area you are responsible for. Find an area where you would like to make a modest change and consider how the principles above could be applied. If appropriate make and carry through a plan. If the change looks too daunting, look at the section on leading and managing change in Chapter 5 for further ideas.

Living with change and emergent order

Whether or not the churning of repeated reorganisation is a benefit to the health service, it is certainly something that health service managers and clinicians have had to learn to live with over many years. To some extent it can be seen as a consequence of the political imperative to take initiatives designed to win public support (and, perhaps, elections). Some of us may look back with nostalgia on the relatively slow pace of change while the post-war political consensus on the service culture of the NHS held. However, nostalgia is not helpful to those who have to manage within the present context. Perhaps the crisis in financial markets alluded to above will lead to a rethink about the current direction in the English NHS, but it seems unlikely. Either way change seems likely to continue, largely driven by politics and the media as well as by emerging technology. In these circumstances managers have to learn to live with change and to influence it for the benefit of patients.

A key issue here is to resist the feeling of disempowerment that comes with too much centrally directed change. Some years ago it was popular to speak of the 'judo' theory of management where one used the momentum of imposed change to 'throw' things in the direction one wanted them to follow. This is a helpful metaphor for the modern NHS. The medical manager needs to have clear principles and direction (the GMC 'duties of a doctor' make a good starting point). Then, whatever change is imposed, the clear principles and direction can be employed to shift the change in the direction one judges to be in the best interests of patients.

REFERENCES

1 Morgan G. *Images of Organization*. London: Sage Publications; 2006.
2 Handy C. *The Gods of Management*. London: Arrow Business Books; 1995.
3 Department of Health. *Equity and Excellence: liberating the NHS*. London: Department of Health; 2010.

FURTHER READING

• Handy C. *Understanding Organizations*. Rev. ed. London: Penguin; 2005.

CHAPTER 4

Personal vision, values and goals: alignment with the organisation

WHAT'S IMPORTANT TO YOU? DEVELOPING YOUR 'VISION'

Almost all senior doctors are (or should be) involved in management. The degree of involvement will vary from negotiations with colleagues about 'on-call' commitments or service reorganisation/development, through posts with formal responsibility for aspects of management (for example some aspect of service development) to formal appointments with substantial commitment to management (such as clinical directors, medical directors and associate medical directors). If you have taken on a formal management role, ask yourself 'Why?' Be honest! Here are some reasons from our own experience.

➤ A desire to influence the system and make it better for patients.
➤ The fear that somebody else might get the job and not do it as well as you. (This may or may not be true!)
➤ A desire to stop bad decisions being made.
➤ Enjoyment of status, power (and enhanced salary).
➤ A real interest in good leadership and management.
➤ Despair at the perverse effects of repeated health service 'reforms' and the desire to mitigate damage.
➤ Passionate commitment to developing a health market.
➤ Belief that doctors have a very important role to play in the management of health provision.
➤ Conviction that only with the powerful involvement of clinicians will the system serve the needs of patients/service users.
➤ A choice of management as a 'career pathway'.

More senior management roles may be initially for a fixed term or may be on a rolling contract. In any case it is helpful to develop a personal vision for what you want to achieve and to translate this into goals that can be achieved in a reasonable time scale. Even a newly appointed consultant or principal without 'extra' management responsibilities can benefit from being clear about their vision, values and goals for what they want to achieve on the managerial front in their first year or so in post.

CASE STUDY 4.1

One of the authors was asked to support medical management (one day per week) in a PCT that provided mental health services. The medical director (the only substantive psychiatric consultant in post in the whole trust!) had died unexpectedly, following an accident, not long after recruiting several new consultants on short-term contracts from the European Union. The vision was to get the medical aspects of the mental health services working effectively again. There was concordance between the values of the author and that of the organisation that focused on providing first-class services for people with mental health problems and enabling them to contribute fully to their own recovery. This vision broke down into a number of very practical goals, some of which are listed below.

- Support the induction of the new consultants into the trust including an understanding of the organisation of the NHS and the trust, psychiatric practice and mental health legislation in England, etc.
- Establish and implement policies and procedures for medical employment, leave, continuing professional development, appraisal, job planning and performance management, etc. (There were 'legacy' policies from a previous organisational set-up but they did not 'fit' the new organisation.)
- Re-establish the trust as a respected provider of medical education and training.
- Support one locum consultant in gaining access to the specialist register via article 14, a route for non-European qualified specialists and others.
- Develop the consultant workforce to a point where long-term appointments could be made to consultant posts and a substantive medical director for mental health could be appointed from among the consultant body.
- Support the establishment of an enduring culture of cooperation between the medical workforce and the management of the organisation in which the needs of service users were the first priority.

The initial timescale for achieving this was one to two years. This was too ambitious! With an incredible amount of support from the director of mental health services, the chief executive, the medical personnel specialist, administrative and secretarial staff, the consultants themselves and the medical school and deanery, these goals (and a number of other important goals that developed over the period) were all achieved within four years. In addition, the culture of cooperation meant that special interests of consultants were harnessed to improve the service by developing specialist services for people with borderline personality disorder, eating disorders and family therapy.

Not all management appointments will be so time limited or so circumscribed in their intention. Nevertheless, if you have not already done so, it is worth considering your personal vision for what you can achieve in management over a realistic time period. It may be something as limited (but not necessarily easy) as developing a cooperative culture or establishing a good reputation for training, or it may be a 'higher-order' vision like 'getting the medical aspects of the mental health services working effectively again'. Whatever it is, it will need thinking about and priorities and goals will need to be set. Figure 4.1 illustrates this process graphically. The foundation

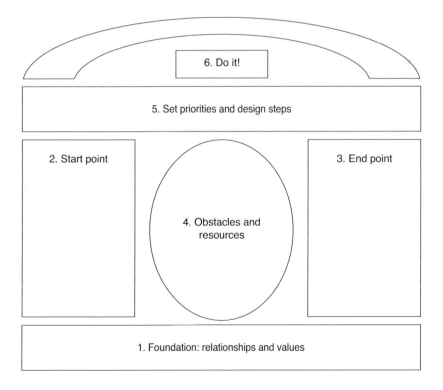

FIGURE 4.1 Planning to achieve your vision or a goal

for any project involving people is relationships and (shared) values. Next comes a realistic appreciation of where we are and where we want to be (the 'vision'). After this it is necessary to consider the possible obstacles and the resources needed to achieve the vision (after which the end point may need to be revised to a more realistic position!). Finally the tasks needed to achieve the goal/vision need to be prioritised and steps need to be designed, ideally with timings sketched in.

EXERCISE 4.1

What is your vision for what you want to achieve in the management field in your current post? (This corresponds to the first of Stephen Covey's *7 Habits*;[1] being proactive prevents the disappointment inherent in always reacting to other people's initiatives.) State this vision as succinctly as possible and decide on a realistic date for achieving it. (This corresponds to the second habit, 'begin with the end in mind'.) Look at the gap between where you are now and where you want to be. Consider what resources are needed to achieve the change (this may be good quality relationships, alliances and communications as much as, or more than, financial resources.) Think about likely obstacles and how they can be negotiated. Prioritise and break the vision down into goals that are manageable and time-limited. (Third habit: 'first things first'.)

Start progressing towards your goals, keeping a note of what you have achieved in your diary.

WHAT'S IMPORTANT TO YOU? CHECKING YOUR VALUES

We have discussed in an earlier chapter how doctors and managers will share many values as expressed for example in the GMC's ethical code 'Duties of a doctor'.[2] In fact it goes wider than that. When Martin Seligman (known to psychiatrists for developing the 'learned helplessness' model of depression and subsequent work on 'learned optimism') was president of the American Psychological Society, he and his colleagues started out on a project to establish a positive psychology.[3] They looked for a typology of human values and virtues that mirrored the classification of mental disorder. In their project they looked at a variety of cultures, philosophies and religions in an attempt to discover values that were universally (or at least very widely) held in high esteem by different cultures. Twenty-four specific strengths consistently emerged across history and cultures under six broad headings: wisdom, courage, humanity, justice, temperance and transcendence. These are expanded in Box 4.1. They are important because they cause us to appreciate that the dominant values of late twentieth-century and early twenty-first-century capitalism (based on an erroneous interpretation by some economic theorists of the Darwinian doctrine of competition and 'survival of the fittest') are not the only values. There is a pervasive cynicism in modern culture that tends to attribute everything to pseudo-Darwinian motives such as status through riches and celebrity to enable men to attract the fittest partners. In fact, as Robert Wright has ably shown in his works *The Moral Animal*[4] and *NonZero*,[5] this is a very simplistic interpretation of both *biological* and *cultural* evolution. The near-universal human strengths recognised by positive psychology are an important reminder of more realistic virtues from which more useful values can be derived. On a quite different basis, a leading economic theorist and architect of Thatcherite policies, Brian Griffiths, argues that markets, too, need a set of values that are independent of the market.[6] He cites, as common values needed to underpin a market economy, principles of justice or fairness, mutual respect or reciprocal regard, stewardship or trusteeship of 'God's creation' and honesty or integrity (which includes truthfulness and reliability).

The values Griffiths and others recognise as essential to a well-functioning market correspond roughly to justice, humanity, courage and transcendence in the Values in Action Institute's list (Box 4.1). Interestingly, the values of temperance and wisdom do not appear in Griffiths' list. Perhaps they should and perhaps, if they did, we could have avoided the market collapse of 2008! Well, this is a practical book, so enough of the values that motivate people *but* they *are* important and foundational to worthwhile human achievement.

BOX 4.1 Modified from the Values in Action (VIA) Institute classification of human strengths (for more detail see www.viacharacter.org/Classification/Classification/tabid/238/Default.aspx)

Wisdom and knowledge: cognitive strengths
- creativity
- curiosity
- judgement and open-mindedness (including thinking critically)
- love of learning
- perspective.

Courage: motional or *motivational* strengths involving exercise of will
- bravery
- perseverance
- honesty
- zest.

Humanity: interpersonal strengths
- capacity to love and be loved
- kindness
- social intelligence (including emotional intelligence).

Justice: civic strengths that underlie healthy community life
- teamwork
- fairness
- leadership.

Temperance: strengths that protect against excess
- forgiveness and mercy
- modesty and humility
- prudence
- self-regulation.

Transcendence: strengths that forge connections and provide meaning
- appreciation of beauty and excellence
- gratitude
- hope
- humour (including playfulness!)
- religiousness and spirituality (linked to meaning and purpose).

MAKING DECISIONS

Doctors are used to making decisions with patients about health, illness and treatment options. They are trained to make decisions rationally and easily as part of their everyday work. The process of decision-making in a medical consultation appears relatively straightforward (*see* Figure 4.2).

In this model good decisions again depend on good relationships (to gather information and build confidence) and shared values (to ensure the doctor is not imposing his or her values on the patient). We all know that the reality is more complicated than this simple model would suggest. For example, information from caregivers and others may not be available. The unconscious patient is not able to convey any information. The thoroughness of physical and mental state examination will depend upon a number of factors including the physical setting and the time available. Investigations available may also be limited by local factors. The doctor's ability to synthesise information and compare it with the knowledge base will depend on

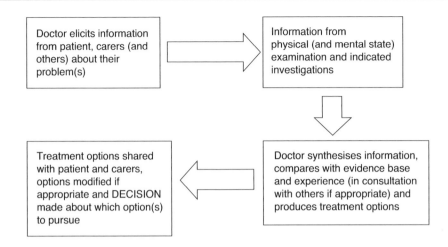

FIGURE 4.2 A simplified model of decision-making in a medical consultation

experience, time, decision-support systems and other factors. Finally, the decision itself may be biased by some factor that has not been taken into account. Perhaps the best treatment option requires a service or medication that is not available (perhaps for reasons of cost), or more time than the patient can spare, or requires giving up some addictive behaviour . . . and so on.

We also know that busy doctors working under pressure take 'shortcuts'. They recognise certain patterns of movement or behaviour and form diagnostic hypotheses as soon as they see the patient. They then proceed to look for evidence to verify the hypothesis. The benefit of this process is that it is often surprisingly accurate and may account for the value doctors put on lots of experience in training and beyond. The danger is that only information that supports the hypothesis is noticed; contrary information may be ignored (confirmation bias) and alternative hypotheses missed.

Individual and collective decisions

In management, decisions often appear to be taken collectively (or not at all!) In truth, decisions are often made by an individual but with the benefit of the advice and support of others. At board level, decisions on important matters are often only taken after extensive discussion, exploration and consultation. In the discussion phase different board members may take opposing points of view, either because of genuine differences or because of the need to 'test' important decisions against possible alternatives. The chairman (usually in conjunction with the chief executive) needs then to find a position that all members are willing to support. Once the decision is taken all members of the board will be expected to support its implementation. There are some similarities between this and a doctor leading a multi-disciplinary meeting to try to find the best available plan to help a patient.

Doctors in management are, however, constantly making more individual decisions, some of which may have a major impact on the future of colleagues or, in extreme cases, the future of the organisation. We are so used to deciding that we do it without thinking (or even realising that we have made a decision). Sometimes we need to stop and take advice before deciding what to do (or not to do). We need to recognise that our decisions are strongly influenced by our values and (sometimes, but not always, inappropriately) our emotions. Below (Box 4.2) is a structure, based on John Whitmore's[7] 'GROW' model for coaching, which can be used to structure decision-making on an individual or a collective basis.

> **BOX 4.2** John Whitmore's coaching model[7] modified as a decision-making tool
>
> **Goal**: What is the purpose of this decision (or this meeting)? What outcomes are desired?
>
> **Reality**: What factors are relevant in this decision? Who else is affected? What are their views (and emotional investment)? How important is this decision to you, to them, to the organisation? What are the relevant values? What are the time constraints? How much priority does this decision have? Are there any stakeholders who should/must be consulted? What resources will be necessary to support the decision and how can they be made available? Are there likely to be any obstacles and how can they be overcome?
>
> **Options**: What are the different options for this decision? Can they be expanded by bringing in other factors? (*See* section on negotiation, Chapter 5.) What are the advantages and disadvantages of each option? Which decision is likely to deliver the best outcomes?
>
> **Will**: What is your decision? To what extent does this meet all your objectives? How will you check whether it has achieved the desired outcomes? What other decisions need to be taken to put this into effect and who will be responsible for carrying them through? (Make sure they are informed and empowered − *see* section on delegation, Chapter 2.)

There are two other factors vital to good decision-making. They are:
1 Proportionality.
2 Appropriate authority.

Proportionality is obvious. For example, we hope nobody would use a tool like that in Box 4.2 when asked if they wanted a cup of tea! Most management decisions do however demand a degree of reflection. *'If you always do what you always did, you'll always get what you always got'* is a wise aphorism. In coaching, a distinction is made between 'reacting' and 'responding'. Reactive decisions over important matters should be avoided. Even in emergency situations reflection can be life-saving. Jonah Lehrer, in his interesting work *The Decisive Moment*, describes a situation in which a fire crew were trapped before a rapidly advancing scrub fire.[8] Most of the crew kept running and were overtaken and consumed by the fire. One, realising he was not going to outrun the fire, stopped, deliberately lit a small fire round himself to burn all the combustible material in the immediate locality and then lay down, allowing the main fire to pass round him. He survived and his practice became a standard part of training for fire crew. The overcoming of his natural tendency for flight and some very quick thinking saved this man's life. The priority and degree of deliberation (not necessarily the length of time!) we give to a decision must be proportional to the importance of that decision.

Appropriate authority is less obvious but equally vital to effective decision-making. It is no good spending a great deal of time and trouble to come to a correct decision if it is actually somebody else's to make. In the clinical situation it is of critical importance that the decision-maker has the appropriate competencies to make the decision. It is a waste of time if decisions are referred to someone who is too senior; and risky if they are made by someone too junior. Though management decisions rarely have the same urgency or the same immediate potential for harm as clinical decisions, the same principles apply.

DIFFICULT CHOICES – WHEN PERSONAL AND ORGANISATIONAL VALUES CLASH

As a doctor–manager you will frequently need to make decisions and choices or to share in collective decision-making and choices. We have already suggested some models for decision-making and emphasised the importance of aligning choices with purpose, vision, values and goals. But what can you do if there is an issue of forced choice? We are all familiar with these in the NHS and they are usually the outcome of economic reality and political theory and practice. The imposition of a pseudo-market on the NHS since the 1990s is a good example. Those who agreed with the political/economic theory had no problem implementing decisions based on this model. Those who had reservations had a difficult decision: Were their values and beliefs so compromised that they had to resign? Was it important to stay in post to mitigate the possible negative effects of the new system?

In making this kind of decision many factors will play a part, including the seniority of the management position held and the views of the rest of the management team.

If there is a serious lack of alignment with local management, the doctor–manager has to decide whether or not they are able to persuade or otherwise influence other members of the team or whether it is more consistent with their own values and integrity to step down. This is the point to discuss influencing skills.

INFLUENCING AND PERSUADING

Influencing and persuading people is an art. But it is also an evidence-based skill. Cialdini describes six universal principles of social influence (Box 4.3).[9] These are based on social psychology research and, although there is some overlap between them, they have an immediate face validity to students of human behaviour. They are also consistent with ideas of reciprocal altruism, based on evolutionary psychology.[4]

BOX 4.3 Cialdini's six principles of social influence[9]

1 **Reciprocation**: We feel obliged to return favours.
2 **Authority**: We look to (trusted) experts, authorities and role models to show the way.
3 **Consistency**: We want to act consistently with our public commitments and values.
4 **Scarcity**: The less available something is the more we tend to want it.
5 **Liking**: The more we like people, the more we want to agree with them.
6 **Social proof**: We look to others to guide our behaviour.

Reciprocation is tied in with a basic human tendency to appreciate 'fair play'. If someone has done something for us we feel obliged to do something for them. Being generous to others predisposes them to be generous to us. In practical terms this means being prepared to do things to support other people when they need our support. A doctor who has 'covered' my on-call at short notice is *more likely*, other things being equal, to receive a sympathetic response if he asks me for 'cover' at short notice. In many ways this is simply a restatement of the ancient principle of 'do unto others as you wish that they would do unto you'.

The role of **authority** is to some extent diminishing in an egalitarian age but we should not underestimate how far people will tend to follow us if they trust our authority and regard us as reliable. To be trusted authorities we need both to be seen to be competent in the area we are to be trusted in and to act with integrity and consistency. It takes time to build this kind of authority as a manager. If we have a reputation for clear thinking, effective communication and wise choices in other fields (for example as clinicians) this may give us a head start. But 'nothing succeeds like success' and people will often wait a while before deciding whether they can trust a new medical manager and whether he or she has carried over skills and aptitudes from the clinical situation.

Because of the way doctors view other doctors, many medical managers find that this trust is better maintained if they retain a clinical input into the service. So continuing in *effective* clinical practice is often seen as a useful way for senior medical managers to maintain their authority and credibility (at least as far as other doctors are concerned). It is worth considering how the different management cultures discussed in the last chapter understand authority. The authority of the 'club culture' derives from connectedness, that of the role culture from organisational position and that of the team culture from knowledge and skills that are useful in addressing the issues the team is tackling. The craft culture likes to be judged by the quality of its work and eschews organisational authority except in the 'master–apprentice' relationship.

Those we seek to influence will have an investment in their own **consistency**. They will tend to stick to their own values, principles and allegiances. Consistency has many aspects in common with the qualities of *congruence* and *integrity* identified as important in successful counselling and coaching relationships (and as part of the VIA set discussed above – Box 4.1). For many reasons it is worth involving one's clinical colleagues in aspects of management and seeking to establish genuinely shared values and principles. If colleagues have learned to be helpful in small matters they will generally be consistent in their helpfulness when larger problems occur. Where there is a tension between beliefs, values and principles on the one hand and behaviours on the other (cognitive dissonance) this creates discomfort. To reduce this discomfort people will generally moderate their behaviour.

Therefore it is important to get active 'sign up' to new ideas or projects from those we want to participate. Once someone has made such a commitment they are more likely to find reasons to support the initiative. Conversely if they are being passively dragged along or acting against their better judgement they are more likely to resist change.

Scarcity is the basis of the science of economics. If something is rare or hard to achieve then it is generally more highly valued and wanted. In getting people to sign up to new ways of doing things, it is good to be able to stress what is uniquely desirable about a particular approach. This often means trying to generate new ideas locally rather than blindly following national policy. Let us be the ones to show how this or that policy can be implemented *really* effectively locally. Being the best has 'scarcity value' so it is a great thing to aim for.

Being liked is something that many of us 'go for' naturally. Being liked and respected is a good foundation for influencing people. We are not thinking here of the 'compulsively' nice person who makes themselves into a doormat for others to tread on. Rather we are thinking of the genuine feelings of affection and mutual respect that people working together to a common cause can achieve. If being genuinely liked helps us influence people, being obnoxious, disliked and not trusted has the opposite effect. It is worth spending time building good quality genuine relationships, not just for their own sake but also for the very practical reason that they will help us when we have to influence or persuade people.

We all like to think of ourselves as independent-minded, especially in Western cultures. However, to a large extent we are validated by the 'norms' of society around us. This desire for **social proof** can produce undesirable as well as desirable behaviour! When we are trying to persuade people to change it helps if we can cite genuine examples of others who have made and benefited from similar changes. Sometimes a successful development elsewhere can be used as a model for new developments; sometimes a local pilot scheme, properly evaluated, can be persuasive.

EXERCISE 4.2

Consider an area where you need to influence people. Be as specific as you can. It may be anything from the adoption of a new assessment form to a radical reorganisation of the service. Decide who are the key people you need to influence. For each person make an inventory from the points in Table 4.1 and think through your answers. Use the answers to decide how you approach those you need to influence on this and future occasions.

TABLE 4.1 Strengthening your position when you need to influence people

Key Point	Question	Answer
Reciprocation	With respect to this issue does this person already feel that I am helpful in taking forward their issues?	
Authority	How does this person view authority and where do they think my authority in this particular area derives from?	
Consistency	How can I present the issue in a way that is consistent with his or her (hopefully shared) values and their commitments?	
Scarcity	Is there some unique benefit for the individual or group in taking this forward? What is it?	
Liking	Does this person like me (!) ?	
Social proof	Are there examples I can give where others have already made similar changes with enthusiasm and success? Will this person be impressed by these examples?	

If you want to maximise your potential to influence other people, you should take careful note of Cialdini's principles. We also need to have confidence in ourselves. Confidence comes with practice, recognising and celebrating success and learning from mistakes. By accelerating this process of celebrating success and learning from mistakes, coaching and mentoring (*see* Chapter 5) may be used to accelerate development of self-confidence and capacity to influence others.

AND FINALLY . . .

Not everything is a resigning issue and certainly anyone who resigned every time he or she had to compromise would not last long in a modern health service. Compromises have to be made all the time but it is important to distinguish those compromises that are *compromising* in the other sense of the word. In other words where they transgress our fundamental values and impeach our integrity. Here, doctor–managers are fortunate. If they have negotiated their contracts carefully and kept up to date clinically they always have the option of reverting to full-time clinical (or clinical and academic) work.

REFERENCES

1 Covey S. *The 7 Habits of Highly Effective People.* London: Simon and Schuster; 2004.
2 The General Medical Council. *Good Medical Practice.* London: GMC; 2006.
3 Seligman M. *Authentic Happiness.* London: Nicholas Brealey Publishing; 2003.
4 Wright R. *The Moral Animal.* London: Abacus; 1994.
5 Wright R. *NonZero.* London: Abacus; 2001.
6 Griffiths B, Sirico R, Barry N *et al. Capitalism, Morality and Markets.* London: Institute of Economic Affairs; 2001.
7 Whitmore J. *Coaching for Performance.* London: Nicholas Brealey Publishing; 2009.
8 Lehrer J. *The Decisive Moment.* Edinburgh: Canongate Books; 2009.
9 Cialdini R. *Influence: the psychology of persuasion.* London: Collins Business; 2007.

CHAPTER 5

People skills

We started by discussing what it takes to get started as a successful medical manager. We have stressed the importance of relationships, of values and of understanding different management cultures in decision-making. We now plan to turn to some specific competencies in more detail.

COMMUNICATION

Communication is often given as the reason for failure. 'Our policies were right but we communicated them badly' is a phrase often repeated by politicians and some senior managers. BP senior management say they were trying to communicate the importance of safety across the organisation when the Gulf of Mexico oil spill occurred. Toyota (more about them later) were seeking to communicate the 'Toyota production method' (and culture) in rapidly expanding international manufacturing plants when they were hit by scandals about faulty accelerator and braking systems. So, what is the essence of communication?

Remember the equation from Chapter 1:

$$\text{Communication} \sim \text{trust} = \text{character} \times \text{competence}$$

In order to 'receive' a communication we have to trust the source in terms of both character and competence. There are other factors, too, including the following.

➤ Communication is essentially two-way (or multi-lateral).
➤ What is said must match what is done (or trust is eroded).
➤ The form of communication must suit the situation.

Communication is essentially two-way

Stephen Covey puts this succinctly in one of his *7 Habits*[1]: Listen *and* be heard. Just as, if we wish to influence people, we need to reciprocate so, if we want people to listen to us, we must listen to them. Doctors and others in the helping professions are taught the skills of empathetic listening. Simply reflecting back the content and emotional tone of what others tell us is a remarkably powerful way of making them feel valued and encouraging them to tell us even more. The authors have lost count of the times when, dealing with a difficult or suspicious patient, they have abandoned the traditional medical interrogation of the patient and switched to empathetic listening as the most effective way of eliciting information. But in management terms, listening is not enough. We also have to be able to make our own ideas heard.

Another idea from coaching is valuable here. It is the distinction between reacting and responding. Sometimes, when we are in conversation, we are constantly reacting to what the other person is saying. A better way is to listen attentively, pause if necessary to consider how their point of view relates to (and perhaps modifies) our own, then give our point of view. Without this consideration of the other person's point of view there is no possibility of a creative synthesis of ideas occurring. While some doctors are too certain that their own point of view is the right one, others (including some doctors in management) are too diffident. We should value our own ideas and seek to create a listening climate in which all points of view can be heard and considered respectfully.

What is said must match what is done

Human beings have very powerful hypocrisy detectors. If what is said does not match what is done, we usually spot this very quickly. The failure may be due to insincerity, poor management or uncontrollable external circumstances; but the dissonance will be noted and likely attributed to insincerity or incompetence, whatever the real reason. Again, this can be understood in evolutionary terms as one of the consequences and conditions of reciprocal altruism. This means that it is very important for any doctor in management to be prepared to deliver what they declare! Sometimes, a failure to deliver will be excused because colleagues understand that unpredictable external events beyond a manager's control are responsible. Some coaches use the aphorism 'under-promise, over-deliver', which emphasises the importance of not undertaking to do something we do not subsequently achieve.

The form of communication must suit the situation

Communicating with the media is very different from communicating with patients, with colleagues or with managers from other disciplines. Character, competence and a respect for the other party are essential in all cases but in other ways, different considerations apply in terms of the following.

➤ Purpose of communication, for example:
  — media
  — court
  — disciplinary
  — public
  — patients and carers.
➤ Language (not just English or other but also appropriateness to the situation in terms of complexity and use of technical terms, acronyms, etc.).
➤ Timing.

Doctors dealing with the media should have special training. This is often a role that falls to doctors in management, especially medical directors. One of the authors remembers attending a media training weekend where a very senior psychiatrist was 'taken apart' in a mock 'hostile interview' by an even more prominent radio journalist. Every media interview should be considered as potentially hostile and the interviewee should go into the interview with a clear idea of the (usually up to three) points they wish to communicate and a determination to give straight answers to reasonable questions. Unreasonable, leading questions designed to show the doctor or his organisation up in a bad light should be firmly, calmly and politely refused or deflected.

Doctors appearing in court should also be trained to deal with potentially hostile questioning from barristers. If they are witnesses to fact they should stick to the simple truth. If they are 'expert' witnesses they should beware of straying outside their field of competence and be humble enough to answer 'I don't know' if they don't. Similar considerations apply in quasi-legal proceedings like disciplinary hearings.

Communicating with the public is often part of the medical manager's job, particularly when there is consultation over planned service changes. In this case there will usually be a communication strategy worked out by specialists in the organisation. This will usually involve several approaches including public meetings and a strategy for communicating via local media. It is important that clinicians in the organisation have an appropriate level of input into such consultations. This means that they need to be involved in planning the changes from the beginning as well as in contributing to any public consultation. Service changes are often resisted, even when they are moving the service in a positive direction. Resistance is likely to be even stronger when the primary reason for changes is cutting expenditure! Nevertheless, this is sometimes necessary and medical managers have to take their part even (or perhaps especially) in controversial consultations.

Communicating with patients and carers is part of every doctor's job. Here the use of understandable (not patronising) language, the recognition that in highly emotional situations communication may have to be repeated, and the value of written information are all recognised. The medical manager is more likely to be involved in communication with patients or relatives if there has been a serious untoward incident or a complaint. Here a genuinely sympathetic attitude is vital, coupled with a rigorous respect for the truth and a recognition that how people perceive a situation depends on where they stand. Timing is important, too. As discussed earlier, a positive and open attitude to dealing informally with questions and complaints at the time they arise may often avoid a more formal complaint being made, involving a great deal of time, investigation and often misery for all concerned. Where there is a formal complaint any investigation and communication of the outcome should be as rapid as possible so that complainants are not kept waiting unnecessarily. When delays are inevitable because of the need to investigate complicated situations or because of the need to conduct legal and/or disciplinary inquiries without prejudice, then complainants should be kept as fully informed as possible about the delays and the reasons for them. Most healthcare organisations will have staff who specialise in managing complaints and will draw in help from medical managers, human resources departments and other doctors when necessary. The complaints staff should also have detailed knowledge of local procedures, time lines and the recording of investigations. They are important allies in supporting medical managers and all those dealing with complaints.

EXERCISE 5.1

Consider the different communications required of you as a medical manager. Which are most important to your success and the success of your organisation? Rank them in order of importance, then in order of the amount of time given to them and then on the confidence you have in communicating in each case. Decide if you need to develop your capacity in any particular area. If you do, include it in your personal development plan.

The special case of email (and other forms of e-communication, including text messaging)

What we have written so far applies mainly to verbal communication, though the same principles apply for written communication. However, nothing about modern communication could be complete without a brief word on the 'splendours and miseries' of e-communication. Table 5.1 lists some of the benefits and pitfalls of e-communication.

One of our colleagues used to say that if she ever reacted to a situation by writing an angry letter she would put it to one side for a day or two and possibly get a respected colleague to read it before it was sent. Nine times out of ten the letter would not be sent or would be heavily modified before it went out! The problem with e-communication is that it is possible to get one's thoughts to other people rather too quickly. Much better to reflect and consult before sending or reacting to an angry email! Because emails do not convey emotional tone in the same way as a face-to-face or telephone conversation, misunderstandings can easily happen with language intended as a 'joke' being perceived as offensive. Generally, confidential information should not be sent by email unless appropriate encryption is used.

Some organisations have policies to reduce information overload, for example by restricting those who can authorise emails with wide circulation. An ideal situation is to have a trusted, reliable and efficient personal assistant with sufficient time to sort incoming emails on behalf of the manager and

TABLE 5.1 Benefits and pitfalls of email and other e-communication

Benefits	Pitfalls
Fast	Fast
Cost effective (apparently)	Information overload (meaning important messages may be overlooked and recipients may be stressed trying to process it all), which can be anything but cost-effective
A 'written record', easy to broadcast, can be used in the courts	A 'written record', easy to broadcast (and copy) leading to over-involvement of people in matters that are not important to them and a potential risk in litigation; risks to confidentiality
Asynchronous	Easy to write and react without due consideration and to pass problems on inappropriately
Informal	Easily misunderstood
'In the moment'	(Potentially) preserved for ever!

prioritise them, even deleting those that are clearly irrelevant. In any case one has to become ruthless in dealing with that which is unimportant but (appears) urgent simply because it appears in the inbox. For more consideration of issues of urgency and importance, *see* the section 'Time management' in this chapter.

NEGOTIATING

Negotiating skills are often identified as a deficit by doctors new to management. In fact it is relatively unusual for doctors in management to be directly involved in formal negotiations. Though they will often contribute to negotiations, for example between commissioners and providers of service, their role will usually be more as technical advisors rather than as direct negotiators. Nevertheless a sound understanding of the principles of negotiation is often very useful in less formal settings. For example a 'job planning interview' with a consultant is essentially a negotiation and many of our conversations with our colleagues, patients and families and carers have elements of negotiation in them.

The authors of *Getting to 'Yes'*, who were themselves part of a major project on negotiation at Harvard University, were involved in real life negotiations in many contexts.[2] Their text speaks from experience, not just theory. They make a vital distinction between *positional* and *principled* negotiation. Positional negotiation is common in everyday life. People take positions (often somewhat extreme) and barter their way to a compromise. Some negotiators are 'hard' in their approach; others are 'soft'. Hard negotiators will often seem to do well but often at the expense of damaging long-term relationships and storing up problems for the future. There are many other reasons why positional bargaining is often inefficient and ineffective. The main points of principled negotiation are summed up in Box 5.1.

BOX 5.1 The main points of principled negotiation[2]

- Separate the PEOPLE from the PROBLEM
- Focus on INTERESTS not POSITIONS
- Invent OPTIONS for MUTUAL gain
- Insist on OBJECTIVE criteria

Separating the people from the problem means working hard not to see our partners in negotiation as 'the other side' or, worse still, 'the enemy'. They are real people too, with their own ambitions, emotions and the agenda of those they represent on their shoulders. The ideal position is to establish a genuine partnership in solving problems for the common benefit.

Concentrating on interests, not positions, facilitates this approach of mutual respect. It is worth trying to find out what the real interests are of any party with whom you are negotiating. Focusing on interests rather than positions makes it easier to satisfy the needs of both parties. Take time to find out what the other parties to a negotiation really want. Make sure they understand what you want, not in terms of a fixed position but in terms of what would really satisfy you or those you represent.

If you know what interests the other party wishes to satisfy, and they know what you want, it is much easier to work together to come up with options. At this stage it is useful to broaden the focus. Are there other factors that can be brought into the situation that will enable more potentially satisfying options to be designed? There should be no premature commitment to any particular option. At this stage all parties should be clear that they are generating ideas, not committing to positions. From these ideas, more new ideas may spring.

When it comes to choosing between options it is best to agree on objective criteria for judging between them. Hopefully it then becomes relatively easy to find one or more options that leave all parties satisfied with the outcome. This is a very brief description of the main points in 'principled negotiation'. The original work[2] goes into each area in considerably more depth and anybody who is likely to be involved personally in negotiation should read it.

EXAMPLE 5.1

A trust wants a high-performing consultant to take on extra leadership and management responsibilities. The trust offers to pay up to two additional sessions in recognition of the extra work. However, the consultant is, in reality, already working a 48-hour week and does not want to extend her hours further. She examines the workload of other doctors in the service and finds that an associate specialist whose clinical judgement she trusts is about to come to the end of a specially funded project working with asylum-seekers one day each week. She discusses matters with him and proposes that he takes on one of her clinics and provides emergency cover for her patients for a full day each week. She suggests to the trust that she would be happy to take the equivalent of one extra session as a (superannuable) 'special responsibility payment'. She suggests that the other session they would have paid her can help resolve the problem of keeping the associate specialist on a full-time contract now that the source of short-term funding has come to an end. The trust agrees.

In this example, all involved have focused on interests rather than positions. It is in the trust's interest to have a doctor working in management and leadership who has genuinely got 'protected' time to devote to this work. By spending less on the consultant's management responsibilities they also find money to help ease the situation of employing the associate specialist five days a week despite the loss of one day's special funding. It is in the Consultant's interest not to be overworked and to have a protected day for her management work. It is in the associate specialist's interest to have new work to replace a short-term project coming to a natural end. Consider also how the consultant has demonstrated her knowledge of the service and suitability for her new role by widening options and finding a new role for the associate specialist one day per week at minimal cost to the trust. Finally, her proposal to take the extra money as a special responsibility allowance reflects reality and ensures that her pension fund is better than it would otherwise have been.

EXERCISE 5.2

Consider an area where you have had to negotiate about funding, pay, medical cover or one of many other possible areas. Was the negotiation conducted as a confrontation between different 'positions' or on a 'principled' basis? Did you follow the guidelines listed in Box 5.1? Did you:
- Separate the PEOPLE from the PROBLEM
- Focus on INTERESTS not POSITIONS
- Invent OPTIONS for MUTUAL gain
- Insist on OBJECTIVE criteria?

How could you have improved your approach to the negotiation? How will you behave differently next time? Try using these principles the next time you are involved in a negotiation.

COOPERATIVE WORKING: COMPLEXITY DEMANDS COOPERATION

Consider how complicated the world has become and how much the practice of medicine has changed in the last 50 years. The older of the authors was taught in medical school by clinicians who had qualified and practiced in the pre-antibiotic era. Pagers ('bleeps') were a recent innovation. Specialist coronary care units were being developed and total hip replacements were a novelty. Computed tomography (CT) scans, nuclear magnetic resonance imaging (NMRI) and numerous other investigatory tools were still a thing of the future and the choice of drugs was extremely limited compared with today's pharmacopoeia. This was just as well since, in the absence of easy access to ready reference tables, interactions between drugs largely had to be memorised! Spending on health was relatively low and the authority of doctors was largely unchallenged.

Now the sheer complexity of the health system demands good management and a culture of cooperation. There is a tendency to 'tribalism' in human nature that sets the interests of our own group against those of other groups. It probably evolved at a time when it significantly enhanced chances of survival. The authors belong to the 'tribe' of old-age psychiatry (and perhaps to the tribes of academia and management as well) and often see our specialty as under-resourced and 'missing out' when special funding comes along. You may belong to the 'tribe' of oncologists, cardiologists, general practitioners, gastroenterologists or one of many others. If you are a medical manager with wider responsibilities you have to put aside your feeling of loyalty to your specialty of origin; or, perhaps better, you need to develop equivalent loyalty to other areas.

Of course, competition is important, too. Politicians sometimes see it as the only way to 'drive change'. This viewpoint is based on the assumption that all who disagree with a particular political theory are curmudgeonly stick-in-the-muds who will resist change. In fact, often services only survive because of the flexibility and cooperation of those who actually do the work with patients. Friendly competition may well be a way of improving standards (for example in clinical audit) but hostile competition is another matter and can be destructive. In our view it has little place in a well-run healthcare system.

ITERATION: MUTUAL UNDERSTANDING, INTEREST AND ENGAGEMENT

Iteration literally means travelling or journeying. In management it reflects the principle that managers should not be 'out of touch' with the parts of the organisation that deliver and support the core business. Sometimes the Boards of organisations will meet on different sites and spend time meeting the workforce and discussing important matters with them. Sometimes individual directors will take an interest in particular functional or geographical units of the service. Senior medical managers need to keep in touch with the work their medical colleagues are involved in. They can do this partly through meetings but these should be supplemented by visits where a proper balance is achieved between informality and reality. We need to avoid the situation where board members either get too optimistic a picture (often when formal presentations are made to them) or too pessimistic a picture (often when someone 'with an axe to grind' overstates problems in the hope of prompting a solution). If the organisation has a culture of honest communication it will be relatively easy to avoid these extremes.

Part of the purpose of iteration is to enable managers to get an accurate picture of the services they manage. Part of the purpose is to develop mutual understanding so that managers appreciate the pressures and complexities of clinical reality and clinicians appreciate the pressures on managers. Medical managers are particularly well placed to promote this mutual understanding as they 'have a foot in both camps'. Finally, iteration can promote engagement. Clinicians (and support service managers) may, once they engage with the realities faced by senior management, be able to offer solutions at no or low cost. Similarly, senior managers, when they understand the problems faced by clinicians and support service managers, may be able to broker solutions, perhaps by small organisational changes (making patient record/computing staff relate more directly to clinicians?).

EXERCISE 5.3

Whatever the level of your management job, consider what steps you need to take to become familiar with the issues facing those you manage (and those who manage you). There are of course many ways of becoming familiar with other people's points of view: listening in meetings, having 'one-to-one' conversations, keeping in touch electronically, etc. But here we are literally concerned with steps – that is physically moving into their situation and perhaps discussing issues face to face in that situation. If you don't do this already, consider whether you might and decide what item of lower priority in your timetable might need to be given less time in order to make the process of iteration a reality.

Finally, if you are a senior manager, remember that being aware of competing needs and priorities in the area you manage may be uncomfortable but it at least enables you to make rational and defensible decisions.

DEVELOPING OTHERS

One of the tasks of any professional is to help develop future and junior members of that profession. For doctors this often means being involved in the education and supervision of medical students and doctors in training.

For medical managers there is also an imperative to develop the management capability and capacity of their doctor colleagues (if only so that they can stand down with an assurance that there is someone competent to take over, in due course). All doctors are, to some extent, involved in management and senior medical managers can develop colleagues' competencies in this area by a variety of means. Delegation has been discussed previously. If colleagues have areas they passionately want to develop (provided the areas are appropriate and acceptable to the organisation) then it is worth giving them support to develop a business case for the development and, if the service commissioner or other organisation agrees to fund the development, helping them develop and manage the implementation of a business plan and project plan to take the development forward. This introduces them to the realities of getting a project funded and of carrying it through to completion. The trust described in Case study 4.1 was strengthened by consultants each having their own area to develop and thus extra and needed services (including a borderline personality disorder service, a family therapy group and a service for people with eating disorders) were provided at minimal cost to the trust.

Feedback from colleagues and 360-degree feedback, if properly managed as part of the appraisal/job planning/personal development cycle is another way of encouraging development of management and leadership skills. This process can also lead to the identification of areas for further development that can be addressed in other ways including:

➤ courses
➤ learning sets and management clubs
➤ coaching and mentoring.

Courses

Management and leadership courses come in many varieties. Sometimes they can be excellent, sometimes they feel like a waste of time and money and sometimes they *are* a waste of time and money! Day release or half-day release courses run by reputable universities and leading to diplomas or even master's degrees in management and leadership can be very valuable for someone new to a senior management post. Short courses, sometimes run on-site by training organisations, can introduce whole groups of doctors to useful concepts. However it is often difficult to judge the quality of such courses in advance. Perhaps the best way of finding whether they meet local needs is to speak to others who have been on them. Distance learning with occasional 'summer schools' or weekends away is another useful way of packaging management training. Before embarking on any costly courses, it is essential to review what is available, to take advice and to count the cost to the person and the organisation in terms of time as well as money.

Learning sets and management clubs

Learning sets, bringing together managers at a similar stage of development, often from different organisations, to discuss and reflect on real-life management issues are valuable and often form part of wider (e.g. day-release) courses. Management clubs more often involve managers at different levels within the same organisation. They may focus on discussing particular issues and some mimic medical journal clubs by trying to find good-quality management research to inform the discussion.

Coaching and mentoring

These are distinct but closely related activities. Coaching is an evolving professional discipline. Coaches are trained to *support people through change, promote a balanced life, accelerate personal development and enable people to realise their potential.* Mentors will tend to be more senior members of the same profession who support junior colleagues by discussing issues with them and sometimes intervening in the organisation on their behalf. Mentors may not have training but when they do, it will often follow similar lines to coach training but not usually in so much detail. Having emphasised the difference it is important to realise that good mentors will often use very similar methods to coaches and that coaches who have appropriate experience will sometimes (subject to the client's agreement) explicitly move into mentoring the client, based on the coach's experience in similar situations. Coaches who do this are usually diligent in being specific about the shift to mentoring and reminding the client that what worked for the coach in a similar situation may not meet the client's needs.

One of the authors is a trained coach and teaches coaching skills to doctors. What follows is a brief description of coaching as presented on the one-day introductory course offered through the Royal College of Psychiatrists Education and Training Centre (CETC; for further details go to their website: www.rcpsych.ac.uk/training/aboutthecetc.aspx).

The International Coach Federation (ICF: www.coachfederation.org/) has described 11 core competencies for coaches in four groups. These are listed in Box 5.2.

BOX 5.2 Coaching core competencies as described by the ICF

1 Setting the foundation
  (i) Meeting ethical guidelines and professional standards
  (ii) Establishing the coaching agreement
2 Co-creating the relationship
  (iii) Establishing trust and intimacy with the client
  (iv) Coaching presence
3 Communicating effectively
  (v) Active listening
  (vi) Powerful questioning
  (vii) Direct communication
4 Facilitating learning and results
  (viii) Creating awareness
  (ix) Designing actions
  (x) Planning and goal setting
  (xi) Managing progress and accountability

Most of these are in familiar areas for doctors. Ethical guidelines and professional standards are similar to those in medicine, with bounded confidentiality and practising within the limits of one's own ability as two examples of standards shared by doctors and coaches. Co-creating the relationship bears some resemblance to what old-fashioned doctors used to call 'bedside manners'. Active listening, powerful questioning and direct communication are areas in which doctors have or should have training. However, in coaching and developmental work generally the *purpose* of questioning is quite different from the usual purpose of questioning in medicine. Medical questioning is usually designed to elicit specific information from the patient that the doctor can use in formulating a diagnosis and treatment plan. In coaching, questions are one of several techniques to increase the client's awareness of the situation they are in and the options they have for action. Again, the action plan should come from the client, not the coach, and responsibility for carrying it through (and any consequences of so doing) rests firmly with the client. It is this shift from the 'expert' or 'medical' model that most doctors find hard to make when learning to coach. Mentoring, of course, does not demand such a radical shift!

As well as core competencies, there are different models for structuring a coaching contract and each session. While, in the opinion of the authors, it is not appropriate for those without rigorous training to set up as coaches and to offer coaching contracts, it is highly appropriate for those with the requisite skills to use coaching competencies and models in helping colleagues develop *their* competencies. This may be done in educational or managerial supervision, or more informally on a peer basis.

We have already discussed Whitmore's 'GROW' model and how it can be applied to decision-making (*see* Chapter 4).[3] When someone comes asking for help or advice on a management (or clinical) issue a similar method can be applied. Ask their permission to use a structured tool. Then ask them, 'What is your Goal with respect to this particular issue?' When this is clear, support them in exploring the Reality of the situation. When all relevant factors have been taken into account, move on to ask them to generate Options for action and to choose which option(s) they Will commit to.

There are many other models and there is only space here to consider one more. This was developed by one of the authors because none of the models he could find stressed the cardinal importance of the *relationship* between coach and client. The method for planning how to achieve a vision or a goal summarised in Figure 4.1 is based upon it. Here it is again (Figure 5.1) in its original form.

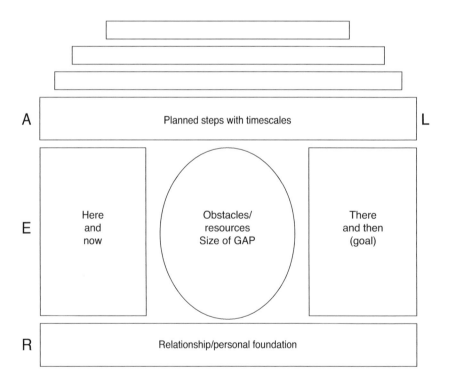

FIGURE 5.1 The 'REAL' model of coaching

In this model, the Relationship between the coach and the coachee and the 'personal foundation' of the coachee are seen as the starting point. 'Personal foundation' is a technical term from coaching that is shorthand for the level of character development of the individual. The next step is Enquiry, to find out about the situation here and now, the desired goal and the size of the gap between them. This stage also includes a consideration of potential obstacles and resources needed and a possible trimming of the goal if it appears unrealistic. Next comes Action, chunking the task into reasonable steps with time scales and finally Learning, when the consequences of the actions are reviewed and any necessary adjustments made. This cycle can be repeated again and again.

In this chapter so far we have discussed some important 'people' skills. They are:

➤ communication
➤ negotiating
➤ developing cooperative culture and the place of competition
➤ iteration, mutual understanding, interest and engagement
➤ developing others through the appraisal/job planning/personal development cycle and through courses, learning sets and coaching and mentoring.

We have given extra space to coaching because we believe it is a foundational skill for a good manager (possibly for a good clinician as well) and because its competencies and models can so easily be adapted to the management situation. We would also strongly suggest that any doctor new to a senior management position would be well advised to seek a good coach or mentor (possibly both). It will help to keep things in proportion and reduce stress. The final issue to discuss here is how to avoid undue stress and how to manage stressful situations when they occur (and they *do* occur).

REDUCING AND MANAGING STRESS

Stress occurs when we feel that we do not have the resources (personal or organisational) to meet targets or standards that are important to us. It is common in healthcare organisations where personal and political aspirations are rarely matched by adequate resources. One of the consequences of long-term stress is 'burn out', a term invented by Cary Cherniss. In her follow-up work, published as *Beyond Burnout* she looked at factors that helped caring professionals prevail in adverse circumstances.[4] These included:

➤ meaningful work that made a significant impact

➤ intellectual stimulation
➤ change
➤ the cultivation of special interests
➤ alignment between individual and organisational needs
➤ greater professional autonomy
➤ support.

The first four of these protective factors are (or should be) available to senior doctors in a well-run service. Alignment between individual and organisational needs has already been discussed as part of the appraisal and job-planning process and in the section on decision-making. Greater professional autonomy is an issue. While senior doctors enjoy more autonomy than most professions working in modern managed healthcare systems, there seems to be constant pressure to erode autonomy through the standardisation (and in some cases the restriction) of practice. Clinical guidelines abound; some are evidence-based, many are based on a balance of scientific evidence and concerns about limiting costs. One of the jobs of medical managers is to seek to protect an appropriate degree of professional autonomy. This not only helps protect clinicians against burn-out, it also enables treatment to be tailored to individual patients in individual situations. Finally, any healthcare organisation should provide appropriate support to its staff, through peer group support and, when appropriate, coaching and/or mentoring.

So much for reducing the impact of 'slow-burning' stress. What about the stress of too much work and impossible deadlines? A number of factors help here:
➤ time management
➤ a balanced life style
➤ appropriate emotional detachment.

Time management
Some of the best ideas in this area come from Stephen Covey and his colleagues.[5] They suggest that we look at our daily work and allocate activities on a grid that separates them into four quadrants:
1 Urgent and Important
2 Not Urgent but Important
3 Urgent but Not Important
4 Not Urgent and Not Important.

Crises and projects and presentations with short deadlines come into the first quadrant. Preventative actions, strategic thinking, relationship-building and thinking about values and how they relate to current reality come in the second. Some meetings, phone calls and emails come in the third, and trivia, junk mail, some phone calls and 'escape activities' (such as playing 'spider solitaire' on the computer) come in quadrant four. It is inevitable that senior managers spend a significant part of their time in quadrant one. Even here, good planning can shift some activities into quadrant two by, for example, starting work well in advance of deadlines. Most people don't spend enough time in quadrant two and Covey and his colleagues argue that this is because of 'urgency addiction'. People allow urgent but unimportant matters to dominate their time budgets. And, of course, they then feel so 'phased out' they waste more time in quadrant four, where computer games and the like give a spurious sense of achievement.

EXERCISE 5.4

Using the grid below, review a day or a week and list where you spend your working time. Try to work out what percentage of your time you spend in each quadrant. According to Covey and colleagues workers in 'high-performance' organisations spend 20–25% of their time in quadrant one, 65–80% of their time in quadrant two, 15% in quadrant three and less than 1% in quadrant four. (They cite corresponding figures for 'typical' organisations as 25–30%, 15%, 50–60% and 2–3%.) How do you and your organisation compare? What can you do to move yourself towards the 'high-performance' end of the spectrum?

	URGENT	NOT URGENT
IMPORTANT	1	2
NOT IMPORTANT	3	4

By removing some of the pressure of the urgent, good time management not only improves performance, it also reduces the stress of feeling there is never enough time to do what needs to be done.

Balanced lifestyle

This is dealt with more fully in Chapter 8. For now, it is important to say that work should never dominate our lives to the detriment of our personal relationships, our wider contribution to society and the meeting of our own legitimate needs.

Appropriate emotional detachment

A balanced lifestyle helps us to maintain an appropriate level of detachment from our work. If we only live to work it is hard to put a proper perspective on problems in the work situation. Of course it is frustrating if a change in economic circumstances or elected government means that an important project is cancelled. But it is not the end of the world. As we get older most of us can look back on problems, failures or reversals that seemed catastrophic at the time (one of us clearly remembers failing to get appointed to an academic chair where he was the only candidate. At the time it seemed *so unfair*! But, soon a visiting professorship was offered elsewhere and that led to the long, enjoyable and reasonably fruitful cooperation between the authors).

So remember, keep things in perspective and when bad things happen repeat one of our favourite aphorisms: 'Worse things happen at sea!'

REFERENCES

1 Covey S. *The 7 Habits of Highly Effective People.* London: Simon and Schuster; 2004.
2 Fisher R, Ury W, Paton B. *Getting to 'Yes': negotiating an agreement without giving in.* London: Random House Business; 2003.
3 Whitmore J. *Coaching for Performance.* London: Nicholas Brealey Publishing; 2009.
4 Cherniss C. *Beyond Burnout: helping teachers, nurses, therapists and lawyers recover from stress and disillusionment.* New York and London: Routledge; 1995.
5 Covey S, Merrill A, Merrill R. *First Things First.* London: Simon and Schuster; 1994.

CHAPTER 6

Organisation skills

INTRODUCTION

In the last chapter we looked predominantly at people skills. Now we want to examine some organisational issues. As we do so it will be apparent that, convenient as it is for heuristic purposes, such a distinction does not really hold water for long!

In this chapter we will examine:

➤ managing and leading meetings
➤ managing and leading change
➤ managing conflict
➤ strategic thinking
➤ business planning
➤ financial control.

MANAGING AND LEADING MEETINGS

It has been said that meetings 'take minutes and waste hours'. Yet meetings are often an important part of health service decision-making processes. Sometimes of course, setting up meetings is a way of avoiding decisions! Also, clinicians, whose main work is in *meeting the needs* of service users, often despair at the plethora of meetings managers call and their apparent inefficiency and ineffectiveness. In a modern healthcare organisation there may also be issues of geographical spread and travelling time. Complex organisations probably do require a certain number of regular meetings but every attempt should be made to reduce the number and duration of meetings by eliminating unnecessary meetings and ensuring that necessary meetings are conducted effectively and efficiently. This may involve setting aside a particular half day when all routine meetings involving consultants are held, perhaps in conjunction with local continuing professional development (CPD) meetings at a common venue, thus reducing time wasted in travelling. Here are some ideas for evaluating the usefulness of routine meetings:

➤ What is the purpose of the meeting (e.g. information sharing, consultation or decision-making)?

➤ What are the alternative methods of achieving this purpose (e.g. a monthly 'news' bulletin, consultation by email or by using a trained interviewer to elicit opinion)?

➤ Are any of them equally or more effective and/or more efficient?

➤ If it is a decision-making meeting does it (or the people attending it) have the authority to make the relevant decisions?

➤ Am I the right person to attend?

When possible more efficient and effective communication and decision-making methods should be used. If there is a genuine need for a meeting then clearly it should be conducted efficiently and effectively. It is essential that a meeting has an end time as well as a beginning. It is then the job of the chair to set an agenda that can be effectively dealt with in the time available. All participants should come to the meeting properly prepared and the chair needs to ensure that an appropriate time is devoted to each item on the agenda. Whenever possible, supporting papers should be circulated in advance. If papers have to be tabled because of urgency they should be brief (no more than one side of A4).

Often the chairing of routine meetings can be used as an opportunity to develop the skills of consultants in this area. It does not all need to be done by doctors with substantial management roles. Whoever chairs the meeting, it is vital that all attending are properly prepared and make constructive contributions that move things forward. Developing a culture that does not tolerate wasting of time in meetings is also important.

In addition to routine meetings, there are also meetings with a fixed life-span to do with managing specific issues or projects. It is important that such meetings are kept to task and that necessary work is done between meetings to carry the work forward. Otherwise the meeting can become a substitute for real work and action and can delay rather than advance the project it is overseeing. It is also important that task-oriented meetings have a clear purpose, appropriate authority and a life that ends when the task is completed (or when it becomes obvious that the task never will be completed). Redundant meetings waste everybody's time. The cost of meetings with senior staff is very significant not only in terms of wasted time (and money) but also in terms of making days more stressful for those whose days are often already more than full.

For smaller task-oriented meetings it increases efficiency if the minutes are kept as action notes and agreed *at the meeting when decisions are made* rather than written up and presented at the next meeting. Action notes should be just that. They should record the agreed decision, the action that flows from it, who has responsibility for the action and a timescale for carrying it through. At the next meeting people should be held to account and asked to report progress (or completion) on the actions agreed at the previous meeting. There is nothing more exasperating than going to an action-orientated meeting and finding that nothing has moved forward since the last one. If that happens one should seriously and openly question the usefulness of the meeting.

EXERCISE 6.1

Look through your diary for the last month and list the meetings you were expected to attend. For each meeting listed make a note of the purpose and whether the meeting achieved its purpose. If you are in a position to do so, question whether there are more efficient and effective ways of achieving the objectives of these meetings. Consider scrapping meetings whose purpose can be better served in other ways. Consider not attending meetings where your presence makes no difference (or perhaps pairing with a trusted colleague so that each of you attends every other meeting). Rigorously examine how each meeting is conducted and whether you could make it more effective and efficient. (This is generally easiest if you chair the meeting; but sometimes possible if you enjoy a good relationship with the chair and can influence them to alter the conduct of the meeting.) Expect this exercise to liberate some time that you can use for other purposes.

When you are in a position to lead meetings (i.e. when you have the chair) it is vital that you set a good example in defining the purpose (and, when appropriate, the authority) of the meeting. You should then structure the meeting to ensure it delivers on its purpose. The Whitmore 'GROW' model[1] has already been mentioned as a useful way of structuring decision-making (Box 4.2). It entails first being clear about the purpose of the meeting and its Goals, then making sure that all aspects of the Reality of the situation are 'on the table'. Then it moves to exploring all the Options for achieving the goals before finally settling on a Will for action (who does what and when by). This, combined with minutes in the form of action notes and a chair who holds people to account for agreed action, can do a lot to improve the efficiency and effectiveness of meetings.

MANAGING AND LEADING CHANGE

Change is an inevitable consequence of being alive. We have already discussed the metaphor of organisation as change and flux in Chapter 3, where we compared the organisation to a self-regulating organism acting as an integral part of the wider system. Change comes from many sources. One useful acronym used to summarise these is used in strategic planning. It is known as STEP analysis and looks at Social, Technological, Economic and Political drivers for change (*see* Box 4.2). Sometimes the letters in STEP are mischievously rearranged as 'PEST', putting the political first, which has certainly been a problem for the UK NHS. Political imperatives have resulted in repeated and frequent reshaping of the parts into new organisations so that some of the natural resilience of human systems has been eroded. One of the authors worked in essentially the same job but as part of three different NHS trusts in three consecutive years! For those working in politicised health systems, this is an expression of the problems caused by *the locus of control being outside the organisation*. At the time of writing, a new government was imposing massive change on the commissioning side of healthcare, allegedly partly under the pressure of *economic* problems. Repeated reorganisation does not seem to be at an end! *Social* change is reflected in demographic changes and changing expectations. Quite apart from this, for all of us, there is the issue of coping with *technologically* driven change.

The *pace* of technological change has been particularly marked in the area of information technology, expressed not only through the internet but also through technical advances in imaging and other areas. Someone once calculated that the volume of medical literature doubles every five years. Even if much of it is not relevant, that kind of exponential change demands effective strategies to ensure that our medical, educational and management practice remains up to date and evidence-based. In the words of one writer we have to adapt from strategies designed for coping in an information desert to strategies designed for coping in an information jungle.[2] *Specialisation* is one way of coping with the complexity generated by such rapid expansion in the knowledge base. *Standardisation* is another one and is the force behind the burgeoning clinical guidelines industry.

The outside *locus of control*, mentioned above, is a particular problem when dealing with a well-educated group like doctors, who function best when given a degree of autonomy. Indeed the latest 'reforms' seem to have given more power back to general practitioners at the expense of PCTs and strategic health authorities.

Standardisation, either in the design of services or in the actual treatment delivered, seems, at first inspection, to mitigate against professional autonomy but this need not be so, provided guidelines remain guidelines and not mandatory instructions. This poses a particular problem where economic issues are dominant. In the authors' own field, the funding of cholinesterase inhibitor drugs for Alzheimer's disease and related disorders comes to mind.

One proposal to deal with the loss of autonomy for hospital doctors was to form partnerships, modelled on the 'chambers' of the legal profession, to sell their services to healthcare providers. While this model might work for essentially episodic and discrete interventions it is unlikely to be able to cope with the demands of long-term and complicated disorders. From the point of view of the government it transfers a lot of the risks (pensions, etc.) to the self-employed doctors. The move to create more 'social enterprises' as healthcare providers is attractive in many ways but it also may involve the transfer of risk (and pension 'funds') from government to smaller enterprises that may be less able to cope with them, especially since current pensions in the public sector are not properly funded but paid from current income. At the other extreme of the political spectrum, it is reported that, in the era of the Soviet Union, cataract operations were 'industrialised' on a 'production line' system with each work station performing a discrete part of the operation. This is essentially a bureaucratic model where each of the workers is a replaceable 'cog' in a machine designed and driven by others. Most of the practice of medicine is not like that, demanding high levels of individual skill and autonomy coupled with effective teamwork.

Assuming that organisations are allowed some continuity and are not broken up for political reasons, how can they best cope with change? (This in the short term at least appears to be the fate of English NHS foundation trusts, which will remain largely intact while the purchasing side is revamped.)

Some change theorists write about dynamic stability. By this they mean that an organisation retains its essential character but makes small, often incremental changes. This is after all the natural way; the way of evolution (which seems to have been remarkably successful!). The idea of dynamic stability can be compared to riding a bike. It is hard not to wobble if you are standing still! By moving at a reasonable speed you achieve stability; but go too fast and there is danger of a crash. If you and your organisation know what you are there for (*purpose*), where you intend to go (*vision*) and how you intend to behave in getting there (*values*) then it will be much harder to deflect you from your objectives. Like a cyclist in a strange land of twisting lanes, you can take a compass bearing on your objective and, whatever the twists and turns of political policy, you can keep on heading for the place where you yourself and your organisation want to be. Pace is important. As noted above, too slow and the cyclist falls off. Too fast and there is risk of an accident!

In Chapter 3 we considered some of the management approaches that are useful in times of complexity and change:

➤ rethinking what we mean by organisations and how they are 'controlled'
➤ learning the art of managing and changing contexts
➤ learning how to use small changes to achieve large effects
➤ living with continual transformation and emergent order
➤ being open to new ideas.

(Adapted from Morgan)[3]

If the change is one you want to achieve rather than one to which you must respond, then these approaches are generally useful. If it is a big change then some further ideas from John Kotter may be of help.[4] He cites eight reasons why organisations fail to change and a corresponding eight-stage process

TABLE 6.1 Eight stages to successful change (modified from Kotter[4])

Eight reasons organisations fail to change	Eight-stage process of 'creating' major change
1 Complacency	1 Establishing a sense of urgency
2 Failing to create a sufficiently powerful guiding coalition	2 Creating the guiding coalition: a team of sufficiently powerful people
3 Underestimating the power of vision	3 Developing a vision and a strategy to carry it out
4 Seriously under-communicating the vision for change	4 Communicating the vision using all means including members of the guiding coalition
5 Allowing obstacles to block the vision (including people, especially senior people, who don't accept it)	5 Empowering broad-based action, getting rid of systems or structures that obstruct the vision
6 Failing to create short-term wins	6 Generating and rewarding short term wins (improvements in performance)
7 Declaring victory too soon	7 Consolidating gains and producing more change
8 Neglecting to anchor changes firmly in the corporate culture	8 Anchoring new approaches by linking to success and development of staff

for 'creating' change (*see* Table 6.1). Please note we have put 'creating' in quotation marks because we would prefer to think of facilitating change in the desired direction as a more accurate description of how things can be influenced in the complexities of the real world. In many healthcare systems the first of the obstacles to change is not so much complacency as weariness with politically directed change. Nevertheless, establishing a sense of urgency remains important. A word of caution here, though: it is better to establish urgency through *vision and desire to be better* than through fear, which is used far too often as a motivating factor by lazy managers (as well as politicians and senior civil servants!). The guiding coalition is vital. Unless you have key people 'on board' you will be 'rowing against the stream'! Communicating a positive vision for change is important even (perhaps especially) when the change is imposed politically. It is only by having a strong vision for the organisation and its future that the impetus of imposed change can be used to move the organisation in the direction of providing better healthcare.

EXERCISE 6.2

Think of some change you want to achieve in your organisation, or think of how you can maintain a healthy organisation, true to its vision and calling during a period of imposed change. Revisit, purpose, vision and values. Consider Morgan's ideas about the 'boundaries' of organisations, changing context, small changes to achieve large effects, living with continual transformation and emergent order and welcoming new ideas! Look at Kotter's eight-stage process and work out how it can be applied in your context. Good luck!

MANAGING CONFLICT

Conflict is unavoidable. However, opportunities for unnecessary conflict can and should be minimised. That is not to say that disagreement should be avoided or dissenting opinions suppressed! An organisation with a clear sense of its purpose and values will be less likely to generate internal and external conflict than one that lacks such clarity. To reduce the likelihood of conflict an organisation and its management needs to adhere to the following principles and behaviours.

➤ Different opinions are sought and valued.
➤ Time is taken to consult and obtain consensus.
➤ The need to deliver care and treatment in a timely way is recognised.
➤ Standards are agreed with practitioners and service users and carers as well as commissioners.

When conflict does occur it should be dealt with quickly and effectively before it has time to develop a self-perpetuating momentum. Where conflict is over a genuine difference of opinion or priorities the principles of *negotiation* (*see* Chapter 5) are most useful. We need to separate the people from the problem and focus on interests not positions. We need to work with the parties to the conflict to look for solutions that are an improvement on the *status quo* for all parties. Finally, in choosing between them we need to devise objective criteria that are acceptable to all. This is no small task and arbitration and conciliation are full-time tasks for some people.

EXERCISE 6.3

Consider an area in which there has been recent (possibly unnecessary) conflict in your area of work. How could it have been prevented? How could lessons learned from this conflict help prevent future problems? Has the conflict been resolved? If so, how? If not, what would it take to resolve the conflict? If you have a current conflict to resolve, apply the principles above and use negotiating skills to see if you can resolve it more effectively.

If you are a manager involved in resolving conflict, it is important not to get 'hooked' into supporting one side over the other. That is not to say that your assessment of the situation is unimportant. You may make a rational decision to support one side but this should not be on the basis of whom you like or find most appealing! A particular feature of some conflicts was described many years ago by Steven Karpman, a transactional analyst who described the 'drama' triangle (also known as the 'victim triangle'), in which people act out their emotional needs in a non-constructive way.[5] The three roles in this triangle are labelled 'victim', 'persecutor' and 'rescuer'. Just as those described as bullies are often the victim of bullying, so those who play the role of persecutor may perceive themselves as victims. Indeed the roles are interchangeable.

CASE STUDY 6.1

A junior doctor complains to the college tutor that the consultant she works for is treating her unfairly. The junior doctor alleges that the consultant is asking her to see too many 'new' patients and has unrealistic expectations of how quickly she can dictate clinic and discharge letters. She is 'at the end of her tether' and tearfully says she is on the point of resigning from the rotation. Because of the perceived urgency of the situation the college tutor (with the agreement of the junior doctor) phones the consultant and asks what is going on. The consultant says she was unaware of any problems. She had been asking the junior to see the same number of new patients each week as the previous junior and had only been trying to maintain the standards demanded by the trust in terms of timeliness of letters. Indeed, the service manager had been putting pressure on her because letters from her team were in danger of breaching trust standards in terms of promptness. She feels she is being put under unreasonable pressure by the tutor and reminds her that her specialty doctor has been off sick for six months, leading to increased pressure on herself. She feels people are making unreasonable demands and threatens to 'take out a grievance'. At this point, the tutor, remembering the 'victim triangle', realises that she has started off by playing rescuer and is now in danger of becoming 'persecutor' while the consultant perceived as persecutor by the junior doctor is in danger of becoming 'victim'. She realises this is a maladaptive dynamic and seeks a more effective way of dealing with the situation.

We have probably all come upon such examples in our daily lives in the highly pressurised atmosphere of providing healthcare. You may want to take a few moments to think of how, in the example above, the clinical tutor could take things forward in a constructive way.

STRATEGIC THINKING

This is a vital function in any organisation (and clearly related to change management and leadership discussed above). The decision-making framework in Figure 4.1 can also be used for strategic planning. A healthcare provider organisation needs to think about its 'customers' and what they are likely to want to purchase over the next planning period (realistically no more than three to five years in the current NHS). The term 'customer' does not sit easily with traditional healthcare practice in the UK. It refers to the patients (service users) but more directly to the people who purchase the services the organisation provides. For GPs, as discussed earlier, this is effectively the patient who elects to use their services. For secondary-care organisations it is likely to be GP consortia purchasing on behalf of patients, though individual treatment and referral decisions may be taken by service users in partnership with their own GPs. Secondary-care organisations are also increasingly likely to need to think how they will 'market' the services they provide in the face of competition from the commercial sector. In fact, a strategy needs many component parts, some of which are listed in Box 6.1.

BOX 6.1 Some component parts of a strategy for a healthcare organisation

- Overall strategy: concerned with the purpose and values of the organisation and where it wants to be in terms of that purpose in (say) three years time. This is really a time limited expression of the purpose, vision and values of a 'mission' statement.
- Product development strategy: how it will develop the range of products needed to maintain or improve its position as a provider.
- Marketing strategy: how it will make sure that purchasers and users of services are well informed about the range and quality of services it provides and the benefits it offers over competitors and how it will keep itself informed about what the purchaser wants and is likely to want in the future.
- Staffing strategy: how it will attract and keep the staff it needs to deliver its core services.
- Quality and effectiveness strategy: how it will set and maintain quality and standards of provision and measure health outcomes.
- Financial strategy: how it will make sure that the financial resources it attracts are sufficient to cover its costs (and make a return for shareholders if it is a commercial organisation).
- Risk-management strategy: how it will manage all kinds of risk, including financial and clinical risk. This may include divesting itself of functions (including some support services) that can be bought in under contractual arrangements that spread risk.

These components are not necessarily all that need to be considered and they can be 'chunked' in different ways (for example financial risk may be considered principally as part of the financial strategy and clinical risk as part of the quality and effectiveness agenda). Some organisations will have a separate 'communications' strategy, others will consider this part of 'marketing'.

Overall strategy

This is really a time-limited expression of the consequences of the purpose, vision and values of a 'mission' statement, which is the foundation on which the whole strategy rests. It includes a realistic assessment of where the organisation is, where it wants to be, what resources it is likely to need to get there and what obstacles stand in the way (including competition from commercial providers who may be willing to undercut the organisation in the short term in order to achieve a greater market share). An estimate that the financial climate is hostile may cause an organisation to 'trim its sails' and have a less ambitious three-year plan, or it may cause it to look for areas where it can bring 'in-house' services that are currently being purchased from other providers at a premium. In mental health, for example, there may be the issue of bringing some secure services currently purchased from a commercial provider into the locality and providing better services at lower cost as part of an overall 'deal' with purchasers. Once all this is carefully assessed, the various component parts of the strategy need to be developed. Two 'tools' mentioned in Chapter 3 are commonly used in constructing a strategy (Table 6.2). One 'STEP' (or 'PEST') analysis looks primarily at the external business environment and has been discussed earlier in this chapter in the context of change management, the other 'SWOT' analysis looks at the organisation itself and the opportunities and threats that the (ever-changing) environment offers and poses.

We considered some of the *social* trends in the UK and European cultures more generally in Chapter 3. In the last 50 years or so we have moved from a 'post-war consensus' about public services and the nature of society to a more strongly capitalist and consumerist position. Centralised planning has become unpopular. Paradoxically, *over-regulation* of public services has become endemic, despite the fact that we are suffering from an *economic* downturn as a result of the 'greed' of *under-regulated* capitalism in areas like banking. The *political* dominance of the capitalist market model seems assured even though its weaknesses have long been known even to its proponents.[6] This is the political economic and social context within which we have to plan. *Technology* is also important in all areas of medicine. This may be high-cost equipment and its use (MRI scanners for example) or expensive new drugs but it may also be the technology of delivering (for example) cognitive behavioural therapy of a good standard to all who need it.

Wishful thinking has no place in strategic planning. Both authors would be more comfortable in a world where the greed and wastefulness of the world's resources that characterise the worst forms of capitalism were less

TABLE 6.2 STEP and SWOT analysis

Social	Strengths
Technological	Weaknesses
Economic	Opportunities
Political	Threats

dominant and where the very rich were not quite so rich and the very poor not quite so poor. Really, this desire for a fairer, more equal society is not just 'wishful thinking'. There is a sound evidence base establishing that more equal societies are healthier in many respects[7]. These ideas can be part of the value system of how an organisation strives to achieve its mission, but no organisation that wants to thrive in a market economy can ignore present reality.

Predicting the future of technology is also notoriously difficult. Not only the technology, but also attitudes towards its use are changing all the time. This is one reason for adopting the relatively short time-horizon of three to five years. Isolation hospitals for smallpox, TB sanatoria and, to a large extent, the old mental hospitals have all disappeared as a result primarily of technological change, though social, economic and political factors have played a part.

In our own specialty, if someone were to invent a drug that halted the progress of Alzheimer's dementia, the whole focus of services would need to shift to the early detection of Alzheimer's disease or, better, the detection of those at immediate risk of developing the disease, so that treatment could be instituted before there was significant brain damage. Such a treatment would also probably reduce lengths of stay in hospital for other conditions quite dramatically, reduce the incidence of delirium and, in the longer term, reduce dramatically the need for residential care. Similarly a medical cure for bowel cancer would dramatically reduce the need for colorectal surgery. These are the kind of things we need to think about.

EXERCISE 6.4A

> If you are in a health provider organisation, spend half an hour thinking through how STEP analysis informs your ideas of what the service will be like in three years' time. If you are a GP you may want to think through how you will be affected as a purchaser as well as a provider of services. If you work in a different healthcare system, adapt the exercise to the needs of your organisation. Consider how much flexibility you need to retain to deal with unanticipated developments.

The next stage is to look at the strengths and weaknesses of your current organisation. Often when people do this they find that some of the weaknesses 'flow' from some of the strengths and vice versa. Try to be realistic and 'hard-nosed' about strengths and weaknesses. If you think your organisation is a pleasant place to work, what is the evidence for that in terms of recruitment, retention, contentment and reduced sick leave in members of staff. In other words, try to find objective data to support your ideas.

EXERCISE 6.4B

So do it! In two columns list the strengths and weaknesses of your organisation (or your part of it). Consider whether and how they make it fit to survive and thrive in its current (ever-changing) environment. Specifically, look at the strengths first and ask how these can be marketed, developed, generalised and otherwise exploited. Many people make the mistake of concentrating only on weaknesses; but often concentrating on building strengths can be more productive. Now look at the areas of weakness. If it were up to you would you want to rectify these areas and if so how would you set about the task? The alternative, if the weakness is in an area that is not part of the core business of the organisation, is to think about whether services could be bought in from another provider or perhaps strengthened by forming a collaboration or consortium with other organisations.

Now you should be in a position to clearly identify the opportunities and threats that the next three years offer to your organisation. How will you seize these opportunities and neutralise the threats? Always bear in mind the need to maintain direction and flexibility even in the face of the relentless change imposed by politicians, technology and social developments.

So that is it – an overview of strategic planning in a nutshell; but it is no accident that this is in the same chapter as change leadership and management and dealing with conflict. They go together!

Product development strategy

This goes hand in hand with marketing strategy; there is no point in developing products (services) that nobody who is in a position to purchase them wants to buy. At the same time, doctors driven by the imperative to provide the best healthcare possible (within available resources) to their population may have strong ideas about services they want to develop. It is very important that the voices of senior clinicians are sufficiently heard in the process of developing services. It is part of the medical director's job to make sure that all senior clinicians (especially doctors) are heard as services are continually redesigned. It is also part of the medical manager's job to offer sound advice to the organisation about priorities, feasibility and *training needs* if new models of service are to be initiated.

CASE STUDY 6.2

A mental health trust decides to institute a functional separation between inpatient and community care. To some extent, this is politically driven by the mandate to introduce 'new ways of working'. Nevertheless, for the general psychiatric services it makes sense because the shrinking bed-base means that there are too many consultant teams working on each ward. By making one or two consultants responsible for inpatients the number of ward rounds is reduced and other consultants spend all or most of their clinical time in the community, where most modern psychiatric care is located, with their teams. The medical manager's job is to anticipate problems (who has authority to admit and discharge, how will continuity of care between hospital and community be achieved? etc.). The medical manager may also need to prevent overenthusiasm for change for change's sake! Do the services for elderly people require the same functional separation? Or does it make more sense with the lower number of consultants, the relatively higher frequency of hospitalisation and the over-riding need for continuity of care to maintain the 'old-fashioned' model of integrated care with the same team providing inpatient and community care? The final answer will differ depending on factors like the size of the area covered, the geographical characteristics of the area, the location of inpatient beds and other issues. The point is that somebody needs to ask the question. That somebody is usually a senior clinician or a medical manager; if it is a senior clinician, the medical manager should take the point seriously and seek to develop a consensus with other senior clinicians about the best way forwards. As far as possible, any consensus should be evidence-based.

Another aspect of 'new ways of working' is that more initial assessments are done in the community by non-medical members of the team. Managers who are not clinicians do not always realise that other disciplines need training and preferably standardised methods of assessment, if they are to make appropriate assessments and recognise those who need urgent action (including referral for urgent psychiatric/medical opinion).

We have drawn this example from mental health services because this is the area with which we are most familiar. We are sure that you will be familiar with other areas of service re-design where only a senior clinician (usually a doctor–manager) can anticipate some of the problems likely to arise and try to ensure these issues are dealt with in advance.

Marketing strategy

A marketing strategy is about many things:

➤ consumer/purchaser awareness
➤ horizon scanning
➤ communication
➤ 'image' or 'brand' awareness
➤ advertising products.

As the health service in the UK becomes more fragmented and commercialised these issues are likely to be of increasing importance.

Consumer/purchaser awareness needs to be developed. In the UK, for the GP the consumer (i.e. patients on the practice list or coming through the door in open access services) is essentially equivalent to the purchaser. For the doctor in a secondary-care trust the purchaser is likely to be a GP choosing on behalf of (or with) the patient. So the provider needs to be aware of what the consumer *wants*. (If, however, the purpose of the organisation is to provide high quality healthcare, not turn a profit, the provider must also take into account what the consumer *needs*, which is not always the same thing.) One way of squaring the circle is to ensure that consumers are well educated so that they understand the difference between wants and needs and know what they need as well as what they want! In a service that strives to provide equitable access there are further problems in that some groups of consumers can be more vocal than others and providing a luxury service for the vocal might mean providing no service at all for relatively undemanding groups like old people. In privately funded services (like those in the USA until very recently) there is the paradox of incredibly good (even excessive) services for the rich and nothing at all for the poor. Nevertheless the principle remains that it is important to have a two-way dialogue with one's patients/customers/consumers/service users/clients!

Horizon scanning is a jargonistic way of saying 'being aware of what's on the way'. This is often particularly hard for clinicians with very busy services. It is hard to 'keep your eyes on the horizon' when 'your nose is to the grindstone'! Scanning the horizon needs to take into account socio-demographic projections (need for more services for older people and for children of immigrants for example), technological innovation, economic projections and the ever-changing face of political fashion.

Communication about the organisation and the services it provides should be part of every marketing strategy. Although the first step is listening, it is also very important to be heard on fair and equitable terms. Organisations that provide healthcare need to communicate not only when things go well, but perhaps even more importantly, to communicate clearly, honestly and with a degree of humility when things go wrong.

This is about maintaining an **'image' or 'brand' awareness** with the local public, purchasers and service users. The idea of working to maintain a public image does not appeal to many doctors and 'branding' is often used commercially to maximise profits from a gullible public. However, if the image offered corresponds to the truth about the organisation (that is if there is integrity in the branding) then it is a way of building public and patient confidence in the provider. Like it or not, public confidence is important.

The GMC has generally taken a dim view of doctors **advertising** to the public and in the UK direct advertising of prescription-only medicines to the public has also been severely limited. However, as providers move into a more commercially oriented marketplace, they will need to learn how to advertise and sell their **products** to purchasers. Part of the story is building good and trusting relationships with purchasers. Being honest, reliable, competitive, well informed and providing consistently high quality services that meet the purchaser's needs is probably the best advert of all; but these qualities need somehow to be brought to the attention of the purchasers who might otherwise not realise what a good deal they are getting.

Of course, product development strategy and marketing strategy are very closely intertwined and some would see product development as part of marketing.

Staffing strategy

There are three elements to any staffing strategy. One is predicting the competencies and therefore the numbers of different types of staff that will be needed in the future. The next is working out how to ensure that sufficient people are trained in each discipline and finally working out how to attract and keep good staff members (which has to do with the culture of the organisation and the quality of its employment practices). Medical managers will most often be concerned with the medical component of a staffing strategy but it will be led by human resources specialists (if the strategy is led at all!).

Quality and effectiveness strategy

These are very important indeed and every organisation needs to have a strategy and a culture that ensures that quality and effectiveness are centre stage. This is the subject of the next chapter so we will not consider it further here.

Financial strategy

Like staffing strategy this is a specialist area best led by finance people. However, finance (like staffing) is a means to the end of providing good healthcare and as such it should not dominate planning but should provide financial boundaries within which service development, marketing, quality and effectiveness need to operate.

Risk-management strategy

Risk management has become a powerful force within business and public services over the last half century. It embraces all areas of function, from finance, to floor polish! Doctors will be most familiar with clinical risk management where the risks of a particular course of treatment or operation are thought through in advance, minimised as far as possible and explained carefully to the patient. However, it also applies to decisions about how many nurses to employ, whether to use locums or agency staff. Doctor–managers will be most concerned about clinical risk management and risk management in areas of medical employment. Although it may be feasible to have a broad risk-management strategy that details the organisation's general approach to the avoidance, minimisation and management of risk, this is also likely to be a 'heading' that has to be considered in other components of strategy.

BUSINESS PLANNING

If the strategic plan for an organisation has a (rolling) three- or five-year horizon, the business plan is much more focussed, dealing with the current year. (Of course ideally it needs to be produced in advance of that year commencing!) Provider organisations usually have an overarching corporate plan and then business plans for each business centre/unit or clinical directorate. Specific projects also need to have a business plan (this has a lot in common with a research protocol but does not go through such stringent ethical scrutiny!). The corporate plan includes the plans of the individual business units/ directorates, takes account of purchasers' intentions and is consistent with the overall strategic plan. It is generally produced over several iterations between purchasers, corporate provider and business units and is sometimes not completed by the time the relevant financial year starts (though it should be!).

Young describes the business plan for a directorate as 'a simple exercise in common sense', which must be consistent with corporate objectives for the year'.[8] He provides a series of helpful questions to consider in developing a business plan as follows.

➤ What is the period to be planned for?
➤ What do we want to do?
➤ What do others want us to do?
➤ What is the probable budget?
➤ How do we integrate these pressures?
➤ What resources will we need?
➤ What will be the effect on other directorates (business units)?

Although the *period to be planned for* is a year, there will usually be a strategic direction over two to three years in order to ensure continuity since many developments take more than a year to realise. *What we want to do* consists of ideas from within the service, for example developing a community service in place of a clinic or training up a group of staff to take on new responsibilities. *What others want us to do* are top-down demands from the organisation and 'sideways' demands from other business units, service users and purchasers. The *probable budget* is hard to estimate and may get harder as purchasing arrangements are again revised. Usually (unless there are major new developments or planned retrenchments) the amount available the previous year is a good starting point with a notional uplift for inflation and some clawed back under the euphemistically termed 'efficiency savings' (Cash Releasing Efficiency Savings – CRES – also sometimes known as 'cost improvement'). *Integrating the pressures* from all these sources requires a lot of time and the involvement of as many people as possible within the business unit. There may be genuine savings that can be made but people will only be willing to bring forward ideas for savings if they can see how they and the unit they work for might benefit. *Resources needed* include staff, finance for recurrent and capital expenditure, services from other business units, and facilities. The *effect on other business units* and, sometimes, on other organisations must also be considered, including costing any extra services needed.

Finally, somebody who is able to write well, who has been involved in the process and has some passion for it needs to sit down and write a draft. Such a draft can be structured into the following sections:
➤ summary
➤ introduction, including how the plan fits into the overall strategy of the unit and organisation and a brief STEP analysis (*see* Table 6.2)
➤ review of last year's plans and achievements
➤ brief SWOT analysis (*see* Table 6.2)
➤ the plan, including how current services will be maintained and how new developments will be progressed, with some details about who will lead and what resources will be needed and where they will come from

➤ how outcomes will be assessed
➤ an appendix of relevant data.

FINANCIAL CONTROL

An organisation, business unit or clinical directorate has a budget to manage. This function is assisted by management accounting. The budget needs to be carefully set in the first place for the whole organisation and for the business units individually. There will be clear rules about whether underspending on revenue can be spent on capital, who can authorise what kind of expenditure, whether and how money can be transferred between budgets, etc. The finance and accounting experts within the organisation will usually produce a forecast of total spend and spend under different headings ('lines') month by month and a monthly review of how spending is going. This gives an opportunity to adjust spending month on month to ensure that targets are met at the end of the year. It is important for the medical manager to be involved in this process since s/he can often help the rest of the team understand why some areas are underspending and others overspending.

This is a very brief introduction to financial control and this area is likely to be of increasing importance in the UK as health services become more commercialised. A more detailed account (including a little about the intricacies of financial and cost accounting) can be found in Young.[8] No doubt more information about how services are to be purchased and how competition will be encouraged in the UK in future will emerge in due course. Decisions about resource allocation between different types of healthcare will have to continue to be made (if only by default) in the emerging marketplace in the UK and it is to be hoped that they will not result in increased inequity.

REFERENCES

1 Whitmore J. *Coaching for Performance.* London: Nicholas Brealey Publishing; 2009.
2 Stewart T. *Intellectual Capital: the new wealth of organizations.* London: Nicholas Brealey Publishing; 1997.
3 Morgan G. *Images of Organization.* London: Sage Publications; 2006.
4 Kotter J. *Leading Change.* Boston: Harvard Business Press; 1996.
5 Karpman S. Fairy tales and script drama analysis. *Transactional Analysis Bulletin.* 1968, **7**(26): 39–44.
6 Griffiths B. *Morality and the Marketplace* 2nd ed. London: Hodder and Stoughton; 1989.

7 Wilkinson R, Pickett K. *The Spirit Level: why equality is better for everyone.* London: Penguin Books; 2010.

8 Young AE. *The Medical Manager: a practical guide for clinicians.* London: BMJ Publishing Group; 2003.

CHAPTER 7

Maintaining and improving quality

There are lots of really powerful examples of things we can do to improve quality while improving productivity.

David Nicholson, NHS Chief Executive[1]

The concept of quality is not an easy one. The White Paper *Equity and Excellence: liberating the NHS* distinguishes three elements of quality: quality of health outcomes, safety and quality of the patient experience.[2] From our point of view, safety can be subsumed under health outcomes and risk management. The quality of the patient experience is itself dependent on health outcomes and other dimensions:

➤ health outcomes (related to evidence-based practice)
➤ relationships
➤ service experienced
➤ management underpinning
➤ timeliness
➤ convenience.

Of course, these dimensions are interrelated to some extent but it is possible, for example, to have a timely, convenient and friendly service that does not produce good health outcomes. If health outcomes are made the primary indicators of quality, then it is likely that to get them right, the other dimensions of quality will also need to be right. Sometimes some aspects of quality have to be reduced in order to provide quantity of service. While this cannot be denied, it is also important to remember that sometimes improving quality can go hand in hand with improved productivity (*see* Case study 7.1 below and quality and productivity case studies on the NHS library website[1]).

EVIDENCE-BASED PRACTICE AND HEALTH OUTCOMES

Good medical practice has always depended on learning from experience and thoughtful reflection. That is why doctors in training are encouraged to follow patients 'through the system' and see what becomes of them. But experience can sometimes be misleading. Why else would the fashion for 'bleeding' patients for all sorts of conditions have persisted so long in earlier times? Routine, valid, clinically relevant and reliable measures of outcomes should be used to ensure services are producing health improvement and to enable any changes in the system to be evaluated. This is quite a tall order! Outcomes are much easier to measure in some areas of medicine than others and persuading people to collect measures that they don't see as relevant is also an uphill and potentially futile struggle. Relating routine outcomes to a reliable and relevant evidence base remains a challenge.

In recent years evidence-based practice has come to rely increasingly on solid scientific methodologies. The most common of these is the systematic review of the evidence for the effectiveness of a particular treatment in a particular condition. For medication the well-conducted, double-blind, randomised, placebo-controlled trial is the 'gold standard' and systematic reviews tend to value this kind of evidence most highly because it is less likely to be biased by human frailty and our tendency to see what we want to see. However, not everybody shares the medical scientist's preference for evidence free from bias and many other kinds of evidence will be brought forward to support particular points of view.

It is part of the role of the medical manager to stress the importance of well-conducted research as a basis for deciding where money should be spent. Not all of this will be double-blind, placebo-controlled, randomised evidence (*see* Case study 7.1). However, whatever the methodology, it should be appropriate to the question asked and the research should be well conducted. Often, on the board or within the directorate/business unit, the medical manager is the person best equipped to make judgements about the quality and relevance of research. This is not the place to go into the details of evidence-based practice. Sackett and colleagues wrote what is still considered to be the authoritative work on the subject in 1996.[3] Readers will be familiar with the method of asking the right question, critically examining the evidence and drawing valid conclusions. They will also know that, in most cases, evidence is examined systematically by organisations like the National Institute for Health and Clinical Excellence (NICE) to produce guidance that is helpful both to managers in making decisions about what services to provide or purchase and to clinicians in their daily work.

EXERCISE 7.1

Look at the area where you have management responsibility. How well (if at all) are the outcomes of interventions measured routinely? How far is the treatment provided evidence-based in terms of NICE or other recognised guidance or in terms of locally agreed evidence-based guidelines? Is there any area in which guidance needs to be implemented? What kind of change in outcomes would you expect? How can they be measured? If necessary you may wish to perform or commission a formal clinical audit to answer some of these questions.

RELATIONSHIPS AND QUALITY

However good the medicine, if the doctor is rude, overbearing, curt and/or uncommunicative, the service user is unlikely to be satisfied. Worse, doctors with poor communication skills may fail to discover what is really bothering the patient and to gather the evidence needed for a sound diagnosis. On top of that, even if the right management is recommended, the service user may fail to follow the recommendations because of lack of trust in the doctor.

The quality of relationships tends to run through a team or organisation. We have probably all been to supermarkets or restaurants where members of staff are obviously disgruntled, often as a result of poor relationships with management. Health services are no different. Staff who are not given due respect and who are treated badly find it hard to treat patients well. There is a lot more about relationships in Chapter 2. They are foundational to a quality service.

SERVICE QUALITY

The quality of a service is essentially a function of the quality of its outcomes, how well it is organised and the quality of relationships within the organisation. How services are organised and the impact this has on the quality of the patient experience is amenable to research. Consumer research asks people what they think of different aspects of the service. Even when patients cannot give a good account of their experience (e.g. people with dementia) methods exist to enable quality to be assessed from the user's point of view (*see* Case study 7.1).

CASE STUDY 7.1

The authors were party to a piece of work that used dementia care mapping to try to understand what made for high-quality ambulance transport for older people with dementia attending routine NHS clinic appointments. The end result was an improved service with escorts, improved understanding of the needs of people with dementia, more attention to their comfort and the avoidance of over long journey times. The new service was also less expensive. This study could never have been conducted using the double blind randomised placebo-controlled trial methodology but the mixed methodology applied was appropriate to the situation and produced worthwhile improvements in quality for patients.[4]

MANAGEMENT QUALITY

The quality of management underpins the quality of the services that an organisation provides. Some of the important aspects of management quality that need to be maintained are as follows.

➤ Creating a culture of mutual respect where good relationships thrive.
➤ Managing finances well so that money is always available to support clinical services.
➤ Managing people well so that the right people are recruited and retained, absenteeism is minimised and the use of locum and agency staff restricted.
➤ Corporate and clinical governance.

The issues of relationships and organisational culture have been explored in some detail in Chapters 2 and 3. Financial management has been discussed briefly in Chapter 6. Managing people well follows from the culture of mutual respect but also requires good administration. Complex issues like on-call rotas, de-synchronisation of annual leave for important staff groups, managing sickness absence, managing study leave and so on call for good administration and procedures that are carried through swiftly and without fear or favour by medical managers and those who assist them. There is also the issue of giving people space to develop their competencies and their own special interests (provided they can be dovetailed with the needs of the organisation and, ultimately, of patients). This will tend to lead to a more satisfied workforce.

Corporate governance is all about the integrity of the organisation and includes areas such as financial control and managers declaring any interests they may have when decisions are being made. Clinical governance is about creating an environment in which clinical excellence can flourish and includes elements of evidence-based practice, risk reduction and management as well as clinical audit and feedback (*see* p. 113).

EXERCISE 7.2

List the ways in which your organisation, or the part of it for which you have responsibility, measures management quality. Some organisations have regular anonymous surveys of staff to discover how well they are doing in maintaining a positive culture. Some organisations have policies for managing sick leave and helping people back to work as soon as possible. The impact of these can be measured by looking at sickness records. Do staff members take adequate amounts of appropriate study leave? Again this can be monitored. Do doctors participate in local continuing professional development (CPD) activities? Is CPD properly supported and monitored to ensure that standards are met? What is the rate of use of locums and agency staff? Is it regularly monitored? Is it satisfactory? What measures can be taken to improve recruitment and retention of permanent staff and how can this be monitored?

TIMELINESS AND CONVENIENCE

When people have a potentially life-threatening illness, timeliness becomes of utmost importance. The right treatment too late is useless. An appointment with a psychiatrist in two weeks or even two days is no use if the patient is severely depressed and acutely suicidal. Likewise, patients with suspected cancer should generally see the appropriate specialist as soon as possible and in any case within a week. For some other conditions convenience will be more important than timeliness. For older people with limited mobility, services provided in the home or as close to it as possible are often more convenient. These things matter to patients and should always be considered when designing services.

EVIDENCE-BASED POLICY

Health policy tends to be based on a different kind of evidence to that which informs the practice of medicine. Comparative studies may show which ways of providing health services are most effective and efficient. Economic and political theories will also often be important in determining the policy framework for publicly funded services. The political theory behind the changes proposed in *Equity and Excellence* for the English part of the British NHS[2] is a particular version of capitalism. It is the same version of capitalism that led to the banking collapse and recession as a result of unbridled greed and under-regulated markets. Hopefully enough has been learned to protect the English NHS from a similar fate!

An area where there is a good basis for evidence-based policy is in the relationship between a more equal society and many measures of health and social well-being.[5] The research summarised in this work shows that, in richer countries, whether lesser degrees of income inequality between the top 20% income and the bottom 20% are achieved by more modest pay at the top or by progressive taxation, health and social outcomes tend to be better. This flies directly in the face of the unbridled capitalism that is politically so strong at present!

One of the jobs of the medical manager is critically to examine policy and ensure that it is not implemented in a naive way. Let us look at two examples from the proposals in *Equity and Excellence: liberating the NHS*.[2]

EXAMPLE 7.1

One of the underpinning values of *Equity and Excellence* is fairness, including a 'ban on age discrimination'. Previous anti-ageism campaigns have led some managers to try to abolish specialist old-age mental health services on the ground that such specialist services are 'ageist'. In fact the reason for the existence of specialist services is that older people with mental health problems have special needs that are best met by specialist services and there is an international evidence-base to support this.

EXAMPLE 7.2

One of the key aspects of *Equity and Excellence* is patient choice and satisfaction. Clearly, even the least sophisticated understanding suggests choices must be bounded by issues of what is clinically effective (and, in a publicly funded service, efficient, too). Yet research shows that doctors can be swayed to prescribe antidepressants wrongly or to prescribe particular brands by patients' expressed views.[6] So, understanding of patient choice has to be modified by what the evidence shows about the effects of patient choice, which may sometimes be misinformed.

Patient satisfaction does correlate with disease outcomes and patient-centred care is associated with lower mortality and fewer complications (and, incidentally, higher cost) in at least one study.[7] One of the factors that influences patients' satisfaction is how their requests for services or products are dealt with. This does not mean that requests must be complied with! Rather, it is suggested that responses that respect the patient perspective are most likely to lead to satisfaction.[6]

EXERCISE 7.3

You may not be part of the English NHS but wherever you are the service you are running is likely to be subject to changes imposed by politicians, insurers or others who have an interest in securing 'value for money' or simply in reducing expenditure. Can you think of any examples similar to those above where too simplistic an understanding of a 'top-down' imperative could lead to negative effects? What evidence can you muster to counteract this possibility? If this is important, can you develop a strategy to communicate this information and to ensure that negative effects are minimised?

In this context, it is also worth considering that The King's Fund investigation into improving the productivity of the health service concluded that *improving clinician performance* through the spread of standardised best practice, not another reorganisation, was the best *evidence-based* way of improving NHS productivity.[8]

RISK REDUCTION AND MANAGEMENT

Safety is a key element of quality and risk reduction is one way of ensuring safety. Doctors tend to focus on clinical risk management. Finance directors focus on financial risk! But there are other risks, too. There are risks to reputation and 'brand' if incidents are badly managed, fire risks if regulations are ignored, health and safety risks if people are not properly trained, and so on. The NHS Litigation Authority (NHSLA) sets and monitors compliance with detailed standards for different healthcare organisations. Table 7.1 is an overview of the risk areas in the NHSLA risk-management standards for mental health and learning disability trusts for 2010/11.

This kind of approach is excellent for an organisation and it is worth working systematically through this chart (or an equivalent one for your type of organisation) to see how it works.

We will not go into great detail here about all the criteria but we will comment on the principles underlying each of the standards in turn. In doing so, we will on occasion go beyond the specific requirements of the NHSLA standards.

TABLE 7.1 NHSLA standards for NHS mental health and learning disability trusts (for more details or other areas, please go to www.nhsla.com/RiskManagement/)

Standard	1	2	3	4	5
Criterion	**Governance**	**Competent and capable workforce**	**Safe environment**	**Clinical care**	**Learning from experience**
1	Risk-management strategy	Corporate induction	Secure environment	Rapid tranquilisation	Clinical audit
2	Policy on procedural documents	Local induction of permanent staff	Sickness absence	Service-user information	Incident reporting
3	Risk management committee(s)	Local induction of temporary staff	Safeguarding adults	Management of service users with a dual diagnosis of mental health problems and substance misuse	Concerns/complaints
4	Risk awareness training for senior management	Clinical supervision	Moving and handling	Health record-keeping standards	Claims
5	Risk-management process	Risk-management training	Slips, trips and falls	Observation of service-users	Investigations
6	Risk register	Training needs analysis	Inoculation incidents	Medicines management	Analysis

Standard	1	2	3	4	5
Criterion	Governance	Competent and capable workforce	Safe environment	Clinical care	Learning from experience
7	Responding to external recommendations specific to the organisation	Clinical risk assessment	Absent without leave (AWOL)	Physical assessment and examination of service users	Improvement
8	Health records management	Hand hygiene training	Harassment and bullying	Resuscitation	*Best practice – NICE*
9	Professional clinical registration	Moving and handling training	Violence and aggression	Infection control	Best practice – national confidential enquiries/ inquiries
10	Employment checks	Supporting staff involved in an incident, complaint or claim	Stress	Discharge/transfer of service users	Being open

*Pilot criteria are denoted with grey shading

Governance

This is the way in which the organisation assures itself and others that it has these matters under control (as far as is humanly possible). It takes an overview, ensuring that senior managers are aware of all kinds of risk the organisation faces and that organisational policies and procedures are in place to minimise risk.

Competent and capable workforce

In many ways this could be considered the most important of the standards. Ideally, simply having a fully competent and capable workforce would ensure all the other standards were met. Proper induction to the organisation and to the locality (including locum staff) is clearly vital. Clinical supervision is also vital and the time will surely come when peer supervision at least is required for all consultant staff and principals in general practice. Interestingly, when medical audit was first introduced, before it transformed into centralised clinical audit, it did serve the function of peer supervision for consultants and their teams. Training in risk management and good arrangements for continuing professional development and training needs analysis are particularly important when people are being asked to acquire or demonstrate new areas of competency (for example in the implementation of 'new ways of working' – *see* Case study 6.2). Training in clinical risk assessment is vital but should not be viewed in too simplistic a way. Experience, general competence in the area under review and detailed knowledge of the patient and his or her condition are at least as important as any of the 'risk assessment' tools currently in use. That is not to downplay the usefulness of such tools whether in assessing risk of pressure sores or self-harm. They are useful and they do remind everybody of the potential risks in particular patient groups; but they are no substitute for proper (multi-disciplinary) assessment by competent clinicians.

EXERCISE 7.4

> Choose an area within your sphere of responsibility and use the applicable NHSLA standards and criteria to assess (from your own perspective) the risk in that area related to the workforce. What are the areas of the greatest concern? Who else is (or should be) concerned about these areas? (Together) what can you do about them? When will you do it? (Use the principles of Figure 4.1 to plan actions.)

Safe environment

Interestingly, for mental health only two or three of the factors listed by NHSLA (slips and falls, 'inoculation' and moving and handling) are primarily to do with the physical environment. The others (sickness absence, harassment and bullying, absence without leave, safeguarding vulnerable people, etc.) are primarily to do with the interpersonal environment, once again emphasising that good relationships and workforce competence and capacity are the keys to all other areas.

Clinical care

This is an interesting list, specific to mental health. The authors would personally want to emphasise the importance of standardised assessment and to add standardised, evidence-based clinical pathways (here as well as in the 'learning from experience' column) to the list. In an age when an increasing number of initial assessments are made not by senior psychiatrists but by members of other disciplines, it seems particularly important to provide a standardised assessment (we *do not* mean a long form to fill in but an agreed set of relevant information that should be collected). As much as possible of the standardised assessment should be filled in automatically at referral (for example, personal and demographic details, past illnesses and current medication). It is wrong to expect clinical staff to spend time filling in data that can be filled in advance of them ever seeing the patient (though of course, risk management demands they should double-check critical data like allergies). Evidence-based pathways are for guidance. They should leave room for negotiation with the patient and variance based upon the knowledge and experience of the clinician. Standardised pathways reduce the risk of error and make it easier to audit the quality of care, both of which are important risk-management objectives. Electronic record systems can be set up to facilitate audit by automatically flagging deviations from the pathway. Remember, though, that a deviation can be for a positive reason as well as a marker of error or omission.

The National Patient Safety Agency (www.npsa.nhs.uk/) is another source of useful advice on clinical risk management.

Learning from experience

Clinical audit

We have given this area its own subheading because we think it is so important and because we think (at least in mental health) it is so badly done. There seem to be two kinds of clinical audit:

➤ Nationally determined standardised audits which conform to nationally defined criteria and which enable comparisons between similar services in different geographical areas. Sadly, these audits often do not fully involve the clinicians and although they provide useful information they only impact on clinical practice indirectly. The Prescribing Observatory for Mental Health in the UK provides a good example of this approach to audit that does have an impact on clinicians.[9]

➤ Locally determined audits (which may use nationally agreed criteria or local criteria or a mixture of both). These audits more often directly involve clinical teams and are more likely to have a direct impact on clinical practice. Even these audits have often been taken out of the hands of clinicians, being performed (rather than supported by) audit 'departments'.

We have been involved in locally determined audits where there was a genuine competition between clinical teams to improve standards. We have not seen this with nationally determined audits. Perhaps the plan, in the English NHS, to give more power to clinicians will result in a more local clinically driven type of audit (ideally incorporating national standards and led by clinical teams with administrative support). We hope so.

Other criteria for learning from experience

The other criteria speak for themselves. It may be trite but it is true to say that virtually everything that happens is an opportunity for learning. Case conferences and personal reflection on clinical work are obvious examples. Complaints (dealt with in more detail in Chapter 2) are an obvious source of information about things that have (or appear to have) gone wrong. We should also listen to compliments as well as complaints and learn from things that nearly go wrong as well as ones that definitely do!

HEALING WOUNDS

We have added this section because we do not think enough attention is paid to the damage done to organisations by persistent wounds. Complaints, inquiries and other necessary activities are often perceived by staff to be very threatening. The criterion, in the NHSLA standard on the competent and capable workforce, about supporting staff involved in an incident, complaint or claim is incredibly important. After any period of trauma to staff of this nature it is well to have a review of how sore they are left feeling. Clearly if there is blame to be attached and disciplinary action to be taken this is even more difficult. But once the dust has settled and any appropriate action has been taken it is time to draw a line and evaluate the current situation.

Persistent resentments and criticisms help nobody. They should be dealt with. One is reminded of the 'truth and reconciliation' movement in South Africa! This sought to heal the wounds of the apartheid era by bringing the truth into the open on the understanding that acknowledging past mistakes without persecuting the perpetrators was essential to enable the country to put the pain of the apartheid era behind it and make a new start.

REFERENCES

1 NHS library archives. Available online at: www.library.nhs.uk/qipp/ (accessed 20 August 2010).

2 Department of Health. *Equity and Excellence: liberating the NHS.* London: Department of Health; 2010.

3 Sackett D, Richardson S, Roenberg W, *et al. Evidence-based Medicine.* London: Churchill Livingstone; 1996.

4 Roberts N, Curran S, Minogue V, *et al.* A pilot study of the impact of NHS patient transportation on older people with dementia. *Int J Alzheimers Dis.* 2010; doi:104061/2010/348065. Available online at: www.sage-hindawi.com/journals/ijad/2010/348065/ (accessed 31 March 2011).

5 Wilkinson R, Pickett K. *The Spirit Level: why equality is better for everyone.* London: Penguin Books; 2010.

6 Paterniti DA, Fancher TL, Cipri CS, *et al.* Getting to 'no': strategies primary care physicians use to deny patient requests. *Arch Intern Med.* 2010; **170**(4): 381–8.

7 Bechel DL, Myers WA, Smith DG. Does patient-centered care pay off? *Jt Comm J Qual Improv.* 2000; **26**(7): 400–9.

8 Appelby J, Ham C, Imison C *et al. Improving NHS productivity: more with the same, not more of the same.* London: The King's Fund; 2010.

9 Prescribing Observatory for Mental Health (Royal College of Psychiatrists). Available online at: www.rcpsych.ac.uk/quality/quality,accreditationaudit/prescribingobservatorypomh.aspx (accessed 3 January 2011).

CHAPTER 8

Balance

No one ever said on their deathbed, 'I wish I'd spent more time at the office'.
Often repeated saying of uncertain origin

Physician heal thyself.
Proverb quoted by Jesus according to Luke's gospel,
ch. 4, v. 22

YOUR MOST IMPORTANT ASSET IS YOURSELF

Some senior managers succeed in their careers only at the expense of a wrecked personal life. Others wreck their personal lives without being markedly successful at work! Balance is essential if anybody is going to survive and thrive as a medical manager and leader. The practice of medicine is stressful and being a medical manager is probably even more stressful. One maladaptive response to stress is excessive alcohol consumption; another is spending too much time at work while ignoring efficiency and effectiveness. You can probably think of others . . . In this chapter we are going to use some approaches from coaching to demonstrate more adaptive responses.

UNDERSTANDING YOUR OWN NEEDS

Sometimes we suffer from 'superman (or "superwoman") syndrome'. We think we can neglect our own humanity and health needs and still perform at a high level. We may be able to do this for a while in an emergency but trying to do it habitually is a recipe for disaster. So, what are our needs? The same as any human being, doctors and doctor–managers have:

➤ physical needs
➤ emotional and relationship needs
➤ mental and intellectual needs
➤ aesthetic, creative and expressive needs
➤ spiritual needs.

Stephen Covey and colleagues express these same needs in the memorable phrase that people need 'to Live, to Love, to Learn and to Leave a Legacy'![1] In coaching practice, whenever somebody reports they are getting bad-tempered and 'cranky' at work, the coach sees this as a signal that important needs may not be getting met. There are two polar-opposite approaches to needs. At one extreme, people may be obsessed with their needs to the point that they think of little else and make little contribution to society. At the other, people deny their needs and end up feeling very stressed and perhaps using maladaptive coping strategies. In the experience of the authors most doctors and doctor–managers tend to deny their needs, often resulting in under-functioning or unhappiness. For a balanced discussion of this area see pp. 31–75 of *The Self Factor* by Duncan Coppock.[2] According to Coppock, when we recognise that we are being 'driven' or affected by an unmet need, there are two complementary approaches we can take. We can either change our attitude so that the 'need' no longer is so important or we can do what we can to meet the need. Which approach we take depends, to some extent, on the nature of the need and our circumstances at the time. The need to eat an adequate but not excessive diet can, for example, only be put on one side briefly without serious health consequences! The need for exercise however, permits a wider range of adaptive behaviours.

Physical needs

How much time do you give to physical renewal or maintenance? Diet, exercise and rest are all important to our physical and psychological well-being; but how many doctors skip lunch or nibble unhealthy food at their desks rather than taking a proper (if brief) break away from the office, surgery, theatre, ward or consulting room? Exercise is often hard to find time for but there are many ways to approach this. For some, cycling to work at least one or two days per week may be a good option. Even parking the car a good way from the workplace and walking briskly, or using stairs rather than lifts can help. For others being part of a sports or dance team or playing golf or going to the gym may do the trick. The key is finding something that works for you and that you can sustain on a regular basis. What about relaxation and sleep? How many doctor–managers lie awake at night trying to resolve impossible problems? You may need to learn to relax, so that you can keep your blood pressure down and get off to sleep!

Emotional and relationship needs

We have already discussed the importance of good-quality relationships and emotional 'intelligence' in the workplace. Our needs for companionship, fun, mutual understanding, appreciation and respect, and our need to contribute to the well-being of others, extend well beyond the workplace and it is these needs that we want to consider here. By the time they rise to more senior management roles, most doctors will have been in a number of close adult relationships. They may be married; they may have children. These relationships can be a source of great balance and support but they also need input of time and energy to maintain them. We need to be able to give to others and to receive from them. (Covey writes of 'the emotional bank account' – our reciprocal emotional 'credit' line with our partners and others.)[3] In order to give to others we have to have confidence in our own status. If we feel empty, we find it hard to give more. And here lies one of the dangers of a demanding job. If we leave work feeling 'drained' it may be hard to give our partner and/or our children the love they need. By being ever-giving at work we run the risk of becoming ever-needy at home. So we need to make a conscious effort to keep a balance in our lives between work and home. This means that we need to keep work and personal life within explicit boundaries. We need to be explicit with other people at work and at home about setting up agreed boundaries that work for all parties (more detail on this can be found in *The Self Factor*[2]).

Mental and intellectual needs

Sometimes needs are also the basis of values. Intellectual rigour is a value that is important to both of the authors. It is based on a need to understand things thoroughly. This can find expression in scientific research, in teaching, in writing and of course in clinical and managerial work. A number of other needs can be listed in this domain:

➤ stimulation from reading and interaction
➤ satisfying curiosity in a rigorous way
➤ learning new things
➤ solving problems
➤ planning
➤ being in control of one's own life and work
➤ having an ordered existence
➤ the search for meanings.

Most doctors will have spent a good part of their lives reading and interacting with others in order to gain the competencies needed for their work;

but what about reading 'outside the box', not only for recreation but also as a way of throwing new light on our professional lives? Good biographies can be inspirational and books on psychology (and dare we say it, some management books) may help us understand ourselves and our working environment better. Being in control of one's own life and work and having an ordered existence are important needs for many people, and lack of control over one's own life at work (or at home) is a frequent source of stress and unhappiness. Many doctors and doctor–managers will find that their intellectual needs can at least be partly satisfied by properly structuring their time at work. Research and audit are examples of parts of the doctor's work life that can be conducted with intellectual rigour and be a source of new learning and problem solving.

Aesthetic, creative and expressive needs

If you are blessed with creative talent, use it! Some people draw or paint or take wonderful photographs, some sing, dance or play a musical instrument, some write books and develop new ideas. Try not to frustrate such needs through lack of time but seek to devote proper time and attention to them. For some people, simply seeing a great work of art or being in beautiful mountain scenery may satisfy deep aesthetic needs. Here again, some people would link this with a sense of meaning in a separate 'spiritual' domain.

Spiritual needs

These are not recognised by everybody. For some people they may be satisfied by adherence to a formal religion, way or path. For others they may be reclassified into other domains (*see* above). The kind of things that may be included here are:
➤ inspiration
➤ meaning and purpose
➤ quiet connecting time
➤ time in nature
➤ gratitude and celebration
➤ kind actions and generosity of spirit.

Again, for more on this area, the reader is referred to Coppock.[2]

EXERCISE 8.1

Consider your needs. The needs review (Table 8.1) is modified from *The Self Factor* with permission.[2] It should not be seen as a kind of test with psychometric validity. Rather it is an inventory to facilitate the reader making a judgement about how far they are meeting their own needs in different areas. The instructions with the original review are as follows:

> When you have completed the needs review [in Table 8.1], choose two or three [or more] that you would like to meet more fully. For each one ask yourself the following questions and write down your replies:
> - How do I feel when this need is not being met?
> - How do I feel when this need *is* being met?
> - What difference would it make if I took better care of this need?
> - What are the implications if I continue not to take care of it?
> - What would be involved in getting this need met more fully?
> - How would I like things to be in 3 months and what is achievable?
> - What steps can I take this week to start to improve things?
> - What support do I need to make this a sustainable change?
>
> Now start to make changes. Remember that the journey of a thousand miles begins with the first step. So take the first steps now, whether they are baby ones or huge strides . . .

Another way to look at the whole question of needs is to imagine yourself as a huge container. Into the container flow all your energy gains: all the things that sustain you physically, mentally and spiritually. Out of the container flow all the things that take energy out of your personal system. Some of these things are legitimate 'output'; things you want to contribute and achieve for yourself, for your friends and family and for your patients and employers. Some of the output goes down the waste pipe! These 'drains' are activities that do not add to your contribution (spending time doing things that really could and *should* be done by others, for example). Making sure all your needs are met is the way to maximise the inflow. Plugging the drains is the way to ensure maximum contribution and achievement. Using this metaphor emphasises that it is a mistake to neglect the 'input' side of the equation. If we do we soon run out of energy for the outputs!

TABLE 8.1 Needs review (modified from Coppock with permission[2])

	Score each item out of 4 according to how you feel about it and don't compare yourself to how you think it should be.			
Physical needs	Rest and relaxation	_____	Diet	_____
	Exercise	_____	Healthy environment	_____
	Touch and sexuality	_____	**TOTAL**	_____ /20
Emotional and relatedness needs	Companionship	_____	Fun and recreation	_____
	Listening and understanding	_____	Appreciation and respect	_____
	Contributing to others	_____	**TOTAL**	_____ /20
Cognitive and mental needs	Stimulating conversation	_____	Stimulating reading, etc.	_____
	Problem solving	_____	Curiosity/new learning	_____
	Planning, control and order	_____	**TOTAL**	_____ /20

Score each item out of 4 according to how you feel about it and don't compare yourself to how you think it should be.

Aesthetic, creative and expressive needs

Beauty in environment	_____
Creating things or ideas	_____
Making a difference in the world	_____
Appreciating the arts, music, theatre	_____
Self-expression/performance	_____
TOTAL	_____ /20

Spiritual needs

Gratitude/celebration	_____
Time in nature	_____
Kind actions and generosity of spirit	_____
Prayer/meditation/quiet time	_____
Inspiration, meaning and purpose	_____
TOTAL	_____ /20
GRAND TOTAL	_____ /100

EXERCISE 8.2

Energy gains, outputs and drains. Make a list in two columns. In one put the main things that energise you. In the other put the main things that you use your energy on. Start with the main outputs that you want to maintain then draw a line and list underneath it all the things that drain energy unprofitably from your personal system. Your list may look something like Table 8.2.

TABLE 8.2 Energy gains, outputs and drains

Energy gains	Energy output
Personal fitness, diet, exercise, etc.	**Useful outputs**
Family relationships	Clinical work well done
Walking the dog	Management work well done
Doing a really good piece of work thoroughly	Good family relationships
Some friendships in the local club/pub/church, etc.	Keeping fit
	Contribution to running local club, karaoke, church, etc.
Reading a great novel	
Writing a book	Writing a book
	Energy drains
	Using inefficient computer system at work
	Having to do work that should be done by someone else (especially if that work does not demand your unique skills and competencies)
	Reading a badly written report
	Attending useless meetings

One thing is immediately apparent in the above; it is the drains that create the imbalance. Many positive outputs are energising in themselves. Life is not a 'zero-sum game'![4] The next thing is how important it becomes to develop plans to deal with the drains and not simply to put up with them. So, if you have completed this exercise for yourself, make a plan to get rid of the energy drains, starting with the easiest and working systematically through the rest!

THE WORK ENVIRONMENT

This is something many doctors tend to neglect. Perhaps it will be different now we have so many shiny new hospitals but many of us have grown up in a resource-starved NHS where getting an office was an achievement and worrying about it being properly equipped was not at the front of our concerns. Just as the issues of quality for patients can be divided into clinical effectiveness, safety and patient experience, so the issues of the environment for the health-service manager can be divided into:

➤ managerial effectiveness
➤ adequate personal space
➤ health and safety
➤ quality of the manager's experience of working in the organisation.

Managerial effectiveness

This depends on the effectiveness of the organisation, its culture and the technical and administrative support it offers its managers (and clinicians). Enough is now known about appropriate and effective management cultures that any organisation has no excuse for ineffectiveness. How often in the NHS do we still come across inadequate technical and administrative support? Certainly in the mental health sector there is still insufficiently good management of administration. Clinical letters are still not always standardised (either in headings for content or in timeliness) nor is the performance of clerical and administrative staff always properly managed. All these things affect the performance of clinicians and managers.

Adequate personal space

Most people need some place to call their own, even at work. An office that is pleasantly furnished and reasonably quiet is a good starting place. Some people will feel content with a shared office, provided there is easy access to an adequate room for private conversations. Doctors with management roles will often have a separate clinical and managerial office and this helps in separating out management from clinical time by making a physical separation of locations. People vary in how much they personalise their workspace. What is important is to make sure that the arrangements you have help to sustain you and improve your efficiency and effectiveness.

Health and safety

Issues like comfortable chairs that avoid back strain, appropriate desk space and suitably arranged personal computers that provide a comfortable and safe working area *are* important. Most organisations offer a work-station assessment for those who spend a lot of their time at a computer or desk. Simple advice on posture, layout of the work station and suitable chairs can make a positive contribution to well-being and comfort in the workplace. Respect for fire regulations is obviously important. Perhaps less obvious are issues like the risks in home visits, especially 'out of hours', poorly lit car parks, etc.

Quality of experience

This partly depends on organisational culture (ask anyone who has worked in an organisation with a 'bullying culture'[5]) but also on whether the work environment conveys the message that the organisation values the employee. This is something the NHS has historically been notoriously bad about. Even in the last five years one of the authors had reports of a consultant psychiatrist being asked to conduct outpatient consultations in an unconverted bathroom in a 'community outpost'! Office space for managers has traditionally been of a better quality. Perhaps this tells a tale of the relative values ascribed to management and clinical work in the 'new managerialism' era of the NHS. If plurality of providers results in more competition, perhaps this will include competition to provide a high-quality working environment.

EXERCISE 8.3

Conduct an audit of the quality of your workplace experience. Under the headings of Managerial effectiveness, Personal space, Health and safety and Quality of experience, list the things that are good about your situation and the things that need changing. Prioritise the things that need changing and make plans to tackle the priority issues with a timescale. Get started and review progress regularly!

TAKING THE LONGER VIEW

It is tempting always to be dealing with the urgent stuff. This may be genuine urgency, as in the case of clinical emergencies, or manufactured urgency, as in the case of many government-imposed deadlines for change. If, however, we allow all of our time to be taken up with the urgent, we may not find time for those important things that help us to keep going. This applies as much to our needs for a balanced life as to the organisation's need to take a strategic overview. Only if we maintain our own personal fitness and balance can we do our best for the organisation we serve.

LESSONS FROM TOYOTA

Until recently, all the management lessons from Toyota have been positive ones. Their concepts of 'just-in-time' supply of parts, a flexible, involved, empowered production staff and total emphasis on quality have been often admired but rarely successfully replicated. Now there is a new lesson; even one of the best-managed companies in the world can go wrong if it tries to go too far, too fast!

Let us look first at two of the positive lessons.

➤ Planning the workflow properly.

➤ Giving the front-line workforce control of quality and incentives to improve it.

The Toyota manufacturing concept starts with the idea that there should be as few detailed performance targets as possible. The approach is dubbed 'management by means' rather than 'management by results'. Overall targets are set for the company but these are kept to a minimum. Management emphasis is on designing the means of production rather than simply going for 'bottom-line' financial targets. Cars are made to order and as they proceed down the production line each car, by means of sophisticated information control, effectively 'orders' the parts needed for the next stage of manufacture. Stocks of parts are kept to a minimum. Production-line processes are designed with input from those who actually work on the production line and every member of the production team learns the work of the stages of production immediately upstream and downstream. Anybody who thinks of a better way of performing some operation is encouraged to share it and all workers are empowered to stop production if they spot a quality issue. The overall flow of production is maintained by having 'buffer zones' between sections of production so that stopping one section does not stop the whole line. For a much more sophisticated analysis of the Toyota production model see *Profit Beyond Measure.*[6]

EXERCISE 8.4

How could 'management by means' improve the area of work you carry (some) management responsibility for? What are the simple, obvious things that need putting right? Administrative and clerical support and effective, efficient, well-maintained computer systems come to mind, as we write this; but you may have many other suggestions. Choose an area that will make a real difference to performance and develop a change strategy for it, based on the steps in Chapter 6. Turn this into an action plan (preferably one that is resource neutral) and (with the support of other key players) see it through. Then start on the next priority!

The more recent lesson from Toyota is that even an almost uniquely well-managed company can go wrong if it tries to do too much, too quickly. Various safety scares have damaged the reputation of the company but it still seems to be maintaining profitability, demonstrating its underlying resilience. We hope the NHS proves equally resilient in the face of the forced pace of change proposed in *Equity and Excellence*.[7]

KEEPING FRESH

How do you keep up to date as a manager? Lessons from medical CPD would suggest that one good way is to have a 'peer group' of managers who help us to design a personal development plan (PDP). The alternative is to regard the PDP as an output from the annual appraisal process. In clinical work, we find that the peer-group process can be used to feed into and inform the PDP agreed in the annual appraisal. A similar approach seems sensible for our own management development. Of course, defining the 'peer group' may not be that easy. Medical directors may choose to use other board members to form a peer group to support them in understanding what development need they have, or they may have a local cohort of medical directors who can help them. Clinical directors and those in similar roles may band together to better develop their understanding. Often, doctors in management will simply become aware, in the course of their daily work, of areas where they could do with expanding their competencies.

This is the formal way of dealing with personal development needs. Informally, reading good management books (especially ones that are based on some kind of research and that have survived into two or more editions – some of the authors' favourites are cited throughout and appear in the Reference lists at the end of each chapter) and active, intelligent discussion with other managers, medically qualified or not, is useful.

When we discussed developing others in Chapter 5, we discussed three ways of doing so:
1 Courses.
2 Learning sets and management clubs.
3 Coaching and mentoring.

The comments we made there also apply when you are choosing how to meet your own development needs as a manager.

REFLECTION, CONVERSATION AND WRITING

Some would argue that the capacity for reflection is one of the important defining qualities of humanity. When we reflect we effectively carry out a conversation in our own heads! We discuss things with ourselves, taking time to assess the situation we are concerned with, to consider other people's views, ponder alternatives and (when appropriate) to form action plans. Coaching is really just having another person to 'hold the space' and perhaps provide some structure for this conversation. In fact, this 'holding space' for reflection is perhaps the most valuable aspect of coaching. In coaching, however, the conversation is not entirely internal. The coach contributes in many ways including by asking questions, keeping the person to their intention and supporting the formation of action plans. It is amazing how having another person listening but not telling us what they think we should do can help the process.

Another way of helping reflection is to write down our thoughts in a structured way. This includes things like the balance wheel in Chapter 1, the time-management grid in Chapter 5, the use of a structure such as Whitmore's 'GROW' acronym, mentioned in Chapter 4, and keeping a reflective diary (and even writing books!). You may have great skill in reflecting on your experience but if you have not tried working with a coach or writing things down in some structured way, you should think about it (and try it!).

WISDOM

What is wisdom? It is an ability to make decisions, based on knowledge, experience, reflection, sound values and good judgement. It has been prized since ancient times and in the Old Testament King Solomon was famous for it! (It is also in the context of the NHS the name of an organisation providing courses on clinical governance and risk management – www.wisdomnet.co.uk/.) In the setting of NHS management, wisdom often consists in seeing the way through the tangle of political initiatives, bureaucracy, regulation and targets that will deliver, first, what is good for the patient, and second, what is good for the organisation. In an ideal world of course these would be identical but, in our less-than-ideal world, the patient should come first! Wisdom is seen in many behaviours, for example in responding to situations after reflection, not reacting immediately (unless of course an immediate reaction is imperative or life-saving!) Wisdom tends to take account of other people's views and tries to assess how things really are rather than accepting a distorted view fed to it by one party or another.

KNOWING WHEN TO STOP

One aspect of wisdom is knowing when to stop. We are coming to the end of this book. Careers in medical management also come to an end. One of the authors retired from a medical director post in a large community and mental health trust partly because he thought the chief executive of the trust had been badly treated and partly because he couldn't put up any longer with continual political meddling in the NHS. After five years pursuing his career as a clinical academic he 'retired' from clinical work but soon found himself invited to help with medical management in two NHS trusts that had lost their medical directors. Now he is stopping again, but he still coaches and mentors other doctors in management, provides occasional direct medical management support and continues to have an academic interest in old-age psychiatry, medical management and spirituality in healthcare. Knowing when to stop is not easy! One vital aspect for younger medical managers is to make sure that they remain competent clinicians with a guaranteed route back into full-time clinical practice.

Hopefully, some of you reading this are just making a start in medical management and have many years of management development, enjoyment, success (and perhaps a little failure) ahead. We trust you will give yourself to the task in a balanced way that will preserve your sanity, your family relationships and friendships and that you will know when to step off the management 'ride' even if it is not until you retire (or later!).

REFERENCES

1 Covey S, Merrill A, Merrill R. *First Things First: coping with the ever-increasing demands of the workplace.* London: Simon and Schuster; 1999.
2 Coppock D. *The Self Factor.* Findhorn: Findhorn Press; 2005.
3 Covey S. *The 7 Habits of Highly Effective People.* London: Simon and Schuster; 2004.
4 Wright R. *NonZero.* London: Abacus; 2001.
5 Hadikin R. *The Bullying Culture.* 2nd ed. London: Elsevier; 2000.
6 Johnson HT, Broms A. *Profit Beyond Measure.* New York: Simon and Schuster; 2000.
7 Department of Health. *Equity and Excellence: liberating the NHS.* London: Department of Health; 2010.

Index

Note: page numbers in **bold** refer to figures, tables and boxes.